W/  P LIBRARY

D0901301

PRAISE FOR MICHAEL AARON ROCKLAND's

# *AN AMERICAN DIPLOMAT IN FRANCO SPAIN*

Michael Rockland's accounts of his unusual experiences while he and I served with the American Embassy in Spain are amusing and illuminating—the most interesting is his tale of the hydrogen bombs that the U.S. inadvertently dropped on Spain and in the waters off its coast. This book will appeal to American as well as to Spanish audiences.

Ambassador Alexander F. Watson
*Former Assistant Secretary of State*

What pleasure it gives me to encounter an American, a former diplomat, who understands so well our country, past and present, and who is equally at home in the world and language of Cervantes as that of Shakespeare.

Jorge Dezcallar
*Ambassador of Spain to the United States*

Brilliantly funny and magnificently unputdownable for Spaniards and Americans who lived through the last death rattles of Franco's regime. This book is a unique performance and an admirable tribute of love from an American to our country as well as a book that, in comparing and contrasting both countries, uniquely illuminates both Spanish and American culture.

Carmen Manuel
*Professor of American Literature*
*Director of the Javier Coy Press, University of Valencia*

Full of stories, both amusing and of historical significance, Rockland has written a book of cultural contrasts that illuminate Spain and the United States in the 1960s as well as today.

Pilar Piñon
*Executive Director*
*The International Institute of Spain*

There are lives that sound like espionage novels, others that suggest Woody Allen comedies. Michael Aaron Rockland's stories from the time he was a cultural attaché in Madrid do both at the same time. He follows in the footsteps of Washington Irving, Henry Wadsworth Longfellow, and Ernest Hemingway as the latest distinguished American to immerse himself in Spanish culture.

Maria Rosell
*Levante,* January 27, 2012

I have just read your book on Spain, and I enjoyed it so much that I found myself doing something I've never done before: writing to an author simply to thank him. Best book I've read in a long time.

Carlos Sanz
*Spanish historian,* August 31, 2011

Michael Rockland's stories, including the one about the day he spent alone with Martin Luther King in Madrid and another about his involvement in the terrible Palomares incident, when, from an American plane, four hydrogen bombs, luckily unarmed, descended on Spain, are priceless. This is a book every Spaniard and every American should read.

Fernando Navarro
*El Pais,* June 3, 2011

# An American Diplomat
# in Franco Spain

# Works by Michael Aaron Rockland

## Non-Fiction

*Sarmiento's Travels in the United State in 1847*

*America in the Fifties and Sixties: Julian Marias on the United States (editor)*

*The American Jewish Experience in Literature*

*Homes on Wheels*

*Looking for America on the New Jersey Turnpike* (co-authored with Angus Gillespie)

*Snowshoeing Through Sewers*

*What's American About America?*

*Popular Culture: Or Why Study "Trash?"*

*The Jews of New Jersey: A Pictorial History* (co-authored with Patricia Ard)

*The George Washington Bridge: Poetry in Steel*

## Fiction

*A Bliss Case*

*Stones*

## Screenplay

*Three Days on Big City Waters* (co-authored with Charles Woolfolk)

# An
# American Diplomat
# in Franco Spain

Michael Aaron Rockland

H
P
G

HANSEN PUBLISHING GROUP

SOMERSET COUNTY LIBRARY
BRIDGEWATER, NJ 08807

*Adventures of an American Diplomat in Franco Spain* copyright © 2012 by Hansen Publishing Group

19 18 17 16 15 14 13 12          1 2 3 4 5 6

International Standard Book Number: 978-1-60182-304-5

Book design and typography by Jon Hansen

All rights reserved. Except for brief passages quoted in newspaper, magazine, radio or television reviews, no part of this book may be reproduced in any form or by any means, electronic or mechanical, including photocopying or recording, or by an information storage and retrieval system, without permission in writing from the publisher.

Photographs reproduced by permission of the Embassy of the United States of America, Madrid.

Hansen Publishing Group, LLC
302 Ryders Lane
East Brunswick, NJ 08816

http://hansenpublishing.com

Dedicated to my many Spanish friends, who have always made me feel at home in their country. And to my wife, Patricia Ard, and my children—David, Jeffrey, Keren, Kate, and Joshua—all of whom share my affection for Spain.

With sincere thanks as well to Carmen Manuel and Jon Hansen who believed in this book and made it happen on two continents.

# Table of Contents

# An American Diplomat
# in Franco Spain

The author in front of his house in Madrid (1966).

# Introduction

I FIRST CAME TO KNOW Spain in the mid-1960s when I served as assistant cultural attaché at the American embassy in Madrid. Friends on both sides of the Atlantic have wondered how someone with my politics and interests could have wanted to serve in the United States government. The answer is simple: when John Kennedy, in his inaugural address, said, "Ask not what your country can do for you, ask what you can do for your country," I took him quite literally; I wanted to be part of Kennedy's New Frontier and joined the diplomatic service in 1961, my first post, Argentina. Part of my enthusiasm, no doubt, came from having grown up at a time of great confidence in, and enthusiasm for, the federal government as an agent of meaningful change. My parents believed, and imbued me with these same ideas, that Franklin Roosevelt and the federal government had saved the economy of the United States through the New Deal, had vanquished the Nazis and the Italian and Japanese fascists, and was the great force struggling to put an end to segregation in our country and poverty and disease worldwide.

The fact that I would be entering the United States Information Agency in particular added to my pleasure, for I would be doing cultural work overseas, and what better preparation for representing American society and culture overseas than an M.A. and an A.B.D. (all but dissertation) Ph.D. in American Studies?

Also important was that Edward R. Murrow, America's greatest broadcast journalist (the focus of a movie in recent years, *Good Night and Good Luck*), would be, however distant from my humble station, my boss. A hero who as much as anyone had vanquished the McCarthyism of the 1950s, Murrow, like so many of us attracted to government by Kennedy, had left his normal pursuits—CBS Television—and was now Director of USIA. He would be my boss and Kennedy would be his. Could any young man in his twenties have imagined a more promising situation in which to begin his professional life?

A book also had some influence on my decision to enter the diplomatic service. It was William J. Lederer and Eugene Burdick's 1958 popular, though undistinguished, novel, *The Ugly American*. Taking place somewhere in Asia—though clearly Vietnam was intended—the novel, while suffused with idealism, exposed how poorly prepared American diplomats were for overseas work. They knew neither the language nor were they familiar with the culture where they were posted. I regarded the novel as a personal challenge to prove to foreign peoples that Americans were by no means stupid and unsophisticated, that some of us, at least, were not ugly Americans—though, ironically, the character in the novel known by that name is actually the hero. Years later I would read Graham Greene's brilliant 1954 novel, *The Quiet American*, concerning, in part, America's earliest blunders in Vietnam, and realized that it might have better prepared me for the realities and challenges of the diplomatic service than Lederer and Burdick's book.

But back then USIA and government in general seemed exciting, the place to be. This was before the disillusionments of Vietnam and Watergate and before the assassination of John Kennedy, Robert Kennedy, and Martin Luther King. It was a hopeful time in American life, and I was delighted to be part of it.

I was then, and remain, an American patriot. The only difference is that, back then, I was naively unmindful of my country's imperfections. I firmly believed that we were the good guys and that ours was the very best country in the world. I wholly bought into the myth of American exceptionalism which isn't patriotism but nationalism. I had not yet learned that my country, like any other, could make mistakes and even be capable of great evil.

And I had yet to learn that there were a host of other nations in the world to admire, among them, of course, being Spain. Spain, more than any other country, would prove to be immensely appealing to me, and it remains so to this day.

When I left Spain in the last days of 1967 I was sad, not just because of my affection for that country and pleasure in my work and life there but because my next diplomatic assignment was Vietnam. It was an index to the obsession of the United States with Vietnam that it would want to send someone like me there. For by that time I was virtually a native speaker level in Spanish and had just completed, in my spare time, my doctoral dissertation involving Argentina and the United States (I had been posted to Argentina before Spain). I would have been happy to stay on in Spain indefinitely or to go anywhere in Latin America. The fact that my government insisted on sending me to Vietnam was a page straight out of Joseph Heller's classic novel, *Catch-22*: if you didn't want to go to Vietnam, they would send you there; if you did want to go, they would assume you were crazy and send you elsewhere.

America's obsession with Vietnam took many forms. Our embassy in that small country was by far the largest in the world, and embassies elsewhere were, as a result, managed by skeleton crews of diplomats. It was as if no country really mattered except Vietnam. In recent years a similar absurdity made Iraq the largest United States embassy in the world. In both cases the waste of those wars was echoed by the waste of the time, efforts, and expertise of American diplomats and a deterioration of our relations with the rest of the world.

I could not imagine what a cultural attaché would do in Vietnam during the war. Could I really interest the Vietnamese in American society and culture, talk to them about Mark Twain and jazz, while they were dodging bullets and bombs, many of them ours? And by that time I had begun to see that the war was a tragic mistake.

I also had three little children I was unwilling to abandon in such a dubious cause; diplomats, after the

Tet offensive of early 1968, during which the embassy was overrun by the Viet Cong, could no longer take their families to Saigon.

Finally, I did not wish to devote thirteen months of my life to full immersion study of Vietnamese at the Foreign Service Institute of the Department of State to get myself to the same level in that so very *foreign* language that I had reached after only sixteen weeks of Spanish. I could not imagine many opportunities for using the Vietnamese language outside of Vietnam. My Spanish, on the other hand, has been a source of great richness in my life during and subsequent to my days in the diplomatic service.

So, although I had thought of a career in the diplomatic service, had hoped some day to be an ambassador, I resigned. I did feel a little guilty. This was silly because, not only had I served my country for seven years in the diplomatic service but, earlier, I had been drafted into the United States Navy and had served in my country's military too. I had been trained as a medic and sent to Japan, where I worked at the United States Naval Hospital at Yokosuka in a locked psychiatric ward that treated Navy and Marine mental patients. Twice I had come close to being murdered by crazed patients in that place. "Friendly fire," they might have called it had my attackers succeeded or covered it up completely. In any case, there are no purple hearts when your own side attacks you. I told myself that I didn't owe America anything more, but I still felt that, in resigning from the diplomatic service, I was, somehow, letting my country down.

Later I would see that it was one of the best decisions I've ever made. I had always been conflicted between my political and artistic sides. Circumstances may have forced a choice, but, luckily, more than anything else, I had always wanted to be a writer, and now I would have that chance.

As for my deep affection for Spain, leaving the diplomatic service has not precluded visiting that country whenever I like. I seem to be back in Spain almost every year, invited to lecture or read from my works or on vacation with my family and seeing friends. Spain has been, and remains, a great pleasure to me and a continuous source of adventure. Some of the things that happened to me, especially during my embassy years in Spain, were extraordinary, so I thought it might interest others were I to share these experiences. Hence this book.

The four years I served with the embassy were when my impressions of Spain were freshest and each day a revelation. I hope it is of interest to readers just how Spain appeared to an American over four decades ago. I am sure that my memories of that time are conditioned by my experience of Spain since, but I have tried to focus on the key events of those years as best I remember them. Still, memory is a tricky thing. There is the danger that one remembers what one chooses to remember. And I do write fiction—hopefully not this time.

The Spain I knew then was still very much the Spain of the Franco dictatorship, and the 1960s there were very different from the 1960s in the United

States. Franco had ruled Spain with an iron fist since the end of the Spanish Civil War in 1939, through the years I served in Spain, and until his death in 1975. The government's slogan during my years there was "25 Años de Paz" (Twenty-five Years of Peace). It is true that Spain remained relatively peaceful during those years, but at what cost?

Even so, Spain was an enchanting place for me. American writers have long gone to Spain and been attracted to its culture. It happened to Washington Irving, it happened to Henry Wadsworth Longfellow, it happened to Ernest Hemingway, and, if I may be so bold as to list my own name in such august company, it happened to me. I have traveled the world, lectured in some twenty-five countries, but I always go back to Spain. Were it possible for me to have a second country, I would choose Spain.

Like my own country, Spain had, and has, its obvious defects, but it was in Spain where I learned to enjoy life. *Disfrutar* (to enjoy) is such a beautiful word. In Spain I discovered great food and wine, a dramatic, ever changing landscape, and warm and admirable people. I guess I fell in love with Spain. I daresay that I still am.

# How I Managed Not to Shake Hands with Francisco Franco

S PAIN WAS A PLUM assignment for a young diplomat, but I was not entirely comfortable with it. Friends back in the United States thought I was a bit of a traitor to progressive causes for agreeing to serve in Spain. In their view, an American diplomat in Spain—even one whose work would be entirely cultural—would be automatically implicated in the fascist dictatorship of Francisco Franco.

It mattered little to them that my principal job would be working with the Spanish universities, encouraging the study of the United States there as well as encouraging American scholars to interest themselves in Spain. Nor were they won over when, in 1966, I helped mediate a dispute between an American researcher and the National Library of Spain. The American, browsing through the stacks of the library, had come across two of Leonardo da Vinci's notebooks (dated 1490 and 1505), filled with precious words and drawings of which the library had no knowledge. The American wanted credit for his find (no doubt it would have won him favor back at his university), but the library, embarrassed, wished to hush things up. Working out an agreement that would somehow satisfy both parties was one of the most delicate acts of diplomacy imaginable. And things got even more complicated when *Life* maga-

The author conferring with a government official. To the right is Tom Sorenson, Deputy to Director Edward R. Murrow of the United States Information Agency, who was on an inspection trip. Sorenson was the younger brother of Ted Sorenson, John Kennedy's key adviser and speechwriter.

zine began sniffing around and eventually published a picture story on the notebooks.

But despite the purely cultural nature of my work, my friends back home still thought I must have gone fascist on them. Franco Spain was Franco Spain. Period. And, indeed, Spain at that time was one big "retirement home" for fascists and even actual Nazis. I would occasionally see the Argentine dictator Juan Domingo Peron strolling about the northern reaches of Madrid, wearing a cape and with an entourage of sycophants and bodyguards. This was before he returned to Argentina as supreme leader for the second time. Fulgencio Batista of Cuba was also around. Once, a long, black Cadillac pulled up alongside me on a Madrid street. All doors sprang open as if on springs, and out jumped four guys in black suits who looked like they were fresh from the set of *Planet of the Apes*. I quickly crossed the street to get away from them. The men surveyed the street, each with one hand inside his jacket, where I assumed there were weapons. Satisfied there were no assassins about, the number one gorilla, Batista, got out and, surrounded by his bodyguards, entered a bank. With the Cadillac idling outside, the whole setup looked like a bank robbery.

When I attended a party in a huge apartment on Madrid's main avenue, the Avenida de la Castellana, the beautiful American movie star Ava Gardner was at one end of a long room and Otto Skorzeny, once known as Hitler's favorite soldier, stood smoking at the other end. *Eros* and *Thanatos*. Skorzeny was surrounded by a boisterous group of men who seemed to be laughing at something he had said. Once a member of the Waffen S.S., Skorzeny was best known as the leader of the September 1943 raid to free Benito Mussolini from the mountaintop in the Alps where Italian partisans held him captive. Coming in at night with silent gliders, Skorzeny and his men extracted Mussolini and reinstalled him as leader of the fascist forces of Italy until, in April 1945 he was again captured by partisans and executed.

Skorzeny was living in Spain under Francisco Franco's protection. Historians have since discovered that he was also active in Odessa, code name for the organization that spirited Nazis out of Germany such as Martin Bormann, Hitler's loyal lieutenant, Adolf Eichmann, the architect of the mass murder of European Jews, and Dr. Josef Mengele, the Auschwitz "Angel of Death." Spotting Skorzeny, I gravitated towards the end of the room where Ava Gardner, was standing. I wasn't sure I could control myself in Skorzeny's presence, and I did not wish to make a scene in the home of my Spanish hosts. Besides, I was thrilled to meet Ava. I tried to engage her in conversation, but she was already too drunk for reasonable discourse. She told me that, for a Spaniard, my English was "excellent." I didn't bother to correct her. It was symptomatic of the Spain of those days that Ava Gardner and Otto Skorzeny could be at the same party. Not to mention me. What was *I* doing there?

My next door Madrid neighbors may also have been Nazis. The previous tenant of my house, a major in the United States Air Force who had been stationed at Torrejón Air Base, told me that my neighbors were Romanian Nazis in exile. In the four years I lived next door to these people, we exchanged not one word, though our townhouses shared a party wall. I could occasionally hear them murmuring on the other side, but I never got to ask them the one thing I wanted to know. Nor would I have known how to ask it: *Hi, are you Romanian Nazis?*

My dog, Pipo, inherited from the Air Force officer along with the house, may have known the truth about the folks next door. He and Ngaio, the next door neighbor's dog, spent the better part of the day murderously snarling and barking at each other on either side of the iron fence that separated the two driveways. The noise was intolerable. I imagined Pipo and Ngaio as surrogates for the unexpressed feelings of their respective masters.

This state of affairs continued for three years, until one day Ngaio came around the fence and attacked Pipo in our driveway. This violated the apparent understanding between the dogs: they could bark and snarl and make a fearsome racket, but they were each to remain on their own side of the fence. Ngaio, the younger and stronger of the two (according to another neighbor on my street, Pipo and Ngaio were father and son), quickly got Pipo by the throat. There was a water hose right there, and I turned it on full force. When the cold water failed to separate the antagonists, I picked up a baseball bat one of my children had left in the driveway and, placing it between the two wet, twenty-five pound struggling dogs, lifted them off the ground. This left me with a sore shoulder but forced Ngaio to release Pipo from his death grip. When the dogs fell to the ground I was able to chase Ngaio back to his own side of the fence. This time a powerful stream of water worked fine.

Pipo soon proved he had not forgotten Ngaio's territorial invasion. One evening, several days later, when the two dogs were at it again at the fence, I saw Ngaio suddenly abandon the field of battle and run down his driveway into his basement. I thought it might be a trap not a retreat, but Pipo immediately dashed around the fence and down Ngaio's driveway. I was not far behind. I did not want to enter a neighbor's house unbidden, especially the house of supposed Romanian Nazis, but I needed to extract Pipo.

I entered the basement just in time to see the next door maid come at Pipo with a raised broom. Before the blow could land, Pipo did an astonishing thing. He launched himself through the air like a rocket and, biting the maid's unprotected leg with a single swipe, left her calf hanging by a few tendons. Surprisingly, there was almost no blood, just that calf flapping freely. The maid and I looked at each other in horror.

Telling her that I would take her to the hospital immediately (to my great relief I learned that the alleged Romanian Nazis were not at home; this would not have been the most auspicious occasion to make their acquaintance), I grabbed Pipo with one hand clamping his muzzle shut, the other grasping him under the belly, and ran out of the basement and up the driveway. Or tried to. Ngaio had hold of my ankle with his jaws and front paws. Luckily, I was wearing heavy jeans and substantial socks, so I would only be left with a small scar on my ankle, but I made slow progress up the driveway dragging Ngaio behind me, with Pipo, eyes demonic, struggling to get out of my grip to attack his adversary.

I took the maid to the hospital, waited while her calf was reattached, paid her bill, and gave her $200 in pesetas, which she seemed grateful to receive—amounting then to several months pay—but how does one properly compensate another human being for nearly having their calf torn off by one's dog?

I awaited some note of displeasure from the Romanian Nazis but they remained silent. Nor did I hear from lawyers. In the United States, Pipo would surely have been quarantined, soon after probably gassed as a "vicious dog," and a law suit for millions would have been brought against me. Romanian Nazis or not, I owed my neighbors an apology, and hereby offer it, but, given their advanced age at the time, I doubt they are alive. And I'm sure Ngaio is long gone too.

As for Pipo, I couldn't take another minute of his war with Ngaio. One of them had to go, and I couldn't imagine flipping a coin with my next door neighbors. So, I put an advertisement in the Madrid newspapers the next day: "Loving dog needs new home. Good with children. Very gentle." I said nothing about Pipo's singular talent, when aroused, to launch himself through the air and nearly remove a calf. Okay, I should have said something about that when, two days later, a fellow American family, living outside Madrid in the town of Alcobendas, came for Pipo. But, after all, Pipo had done it only once and only under the stress of his ancient feud with Ngaio. He'd be fine out in the country, I told myself, away from the Romanian Nazis and their crazy dog. Saddened, but relieved, my family and I waved goodbye to Pipo, never to see him again. Things could now settle down.

But they didn't. With Pipo gone, Ngaio took to trotting over to our house every morning and leaving a "deposit" on the marble front steps. The first few times Ngaio did this, I just cleaned it up. I was still feeling badly about the maid's calf and was not eager to provoke my neighbors. But one day, tired of their dog's misdeeds, I wrote a note and placed it in my neighbors' mailbox. There was no answer and no change in Ngaio's behavior. And marble is a stone that absorbs stains. To make my point more emphatically, I later took to daily scooping up their dog's excrement in a dustpan and placing it on my neighbor's identical marble steps. After a few days, Ngaio stopped coming over. Just how this was managed I never knew. But Ngaio still hung out by the fence between the two properties, looking, I thought, rather forlorn. His *raison d'etre* was gone. I suspect he missed Pipo as much as we did. Maybe more.

I never ascertained the identity of my neighbors. Whether they were Romanian Nazis remains unknown to me. But the fact I had been told they were, and believed they were, was symptomatic of Franco Spain, where such people were in plentiful supply.

Speaking of Franco, I have barely said a word about him yet. I had a Franco-related experience when passing through the city of Caceres en route to a brief vacation in Portugal. Walking around the town, I passed a vast house, so big you could drive cars into its dark interior courtyard. Suddenly, out of the gloom, a voice went "Pssst!" I stopped, and a short man in humble clothes came out into the sunshine and said, "Would you like to see some pictures?" My first thought was that he must have something pornographic in mind.

Instead, this man, who seemed to be a portero (a combination doorman and janitor), had a large cardboard box full of loose snapshots of Franco and his family during the Civil War. I gathered from the man that the Generalisimo had been headquartered in this house in Caceres in 1936 early in the Civil War, but why hadn't he or his family or someone on his staff taken the pictures with them when they left? And it was now decades later. I've always wondered what happened to that box of photographs which, despite my aversion to Franco, must have had considerable historic significance. Perhaps they are still there in that house for a Spanish scholar to discover one day.

I first saw Franco himself one July 18th in the parade on Madrid's Avenida de la Castellana commemorating El Dia del Lanzamiento, the start of the Spanish Civil War, then a national holiday. He stood in an open car, with the young Prince (now king) Juan Carlos beside him, the car surrounded by masses of marching troops and brass bands.

Despite these minor experiences, I never thought I would meet Franco. My official duties would not require me to do so; I was also too low ranking to represent the embassy with anyone high up in the Spanish government. Then, one day in 1967 our ambassador received an invitation to the inauguration of the Spanish National Art Show which took place annually in the Crystal Palace in Retiro Park. This event being of little significance to the ambassador, he passed the invitation on to his second in command. The minister looked it over and passed it on to the director of public affairs. The director of public affairs considered it unworthy of his attention and passed it on to the cultural attaché, and the cultural attaché, my immediate boss, passed it on to me, the most junior of his three assistant cultural attachés. Since there was no one lower than me in the embassy hierarchy to whom I could pass the invitation, I attended the event.

I really didn't mind. Many of my Spanish friends were artists, and I thought I might see some of them there; my work was cultural, after all. But when I arrived at the Crystal Palace there was not one artist in sight. I suppose artists were, by the "wisdom" of Franco Spain, too "subversive" to appear at such occasions even though it was their pictures that adorned the walls. There were, instead, a multitude of Spanish government officials and military officers as well as delegates from each embassy accredited to the Spanish government. Some embassies, representing small countries, consisted of a single diplomat, the ambassador. I rather liked hobnobbing with all those ambassadors.

We diplomats were milling about, perfunctorily gazing at the pictures, drinking wine, and plucking hors d'ouvres from the trays of elegantly dressed waiters, when someone—he must have been the Spanish chief of protocol—announced that we were to form a single line side by side. I found myself situated between the Ambassador of Guatemala and the Ambassador of an African country I had never heard of. I chatted with both of them, but they seemed unhappy to learn that I was not an ambassador but a low, indeed the lowest, ranking diplomat at the American Embassy.

In any case, our socializing abruptly stopped when silence fell over the hall. I looked down the long line of diplomats and nearly fainted. Coming along in military dress, surrounded by various dignitaries, was "the mummy" (as Franco was then referred to by my Spanish friends) himself. He was stopping in front of each diplomat, shaking hands, and exchanging a few words. Some of the diplomats bowed slightly as they addressed the Generalisimo. "Oh, shit," I thought to myself. "What do I do now?"

My embassy work was with intellectuals, people in the arts, university professors and students who represented the future of a democratic Spain. I used to invite such people over to my house and sometimes we would, very quietly to be sure, listen to a collection of 78 rpm records an uncle had given me that had been produced by Republicans during the Spanish Civil War.

The small collection of records was titled "Songs of the International Brigades" and had been recorded in Barcelona. Each had a little paper sticker on it that said in Spanish: "The defects of this record are due to the fact that it was recorded during cuts in electricity during a bombardment." Songs included were "The Four Generals," which parodied Franco and his three leading confederates and songs such as The Thaelmann Column, sung by the German Socialist entertainer, Ernst Busch, who had fled Nazi Germany and joined the International Brigades.

My work in Spain was, I suppose, subversive of the Franco regime in minor ways. Sometimes I wondered whether I might one day step over the line, be declared *persona non grata,* and ordered to leave Spain. The United States government maintained excellent official relations with the Franco government, for, without them, we would not have had the vital military bases in Spain arranged during the Eisenhower administration. Culture, what I did, was all very well, but it would never be allowed to undermine military arrangements. The Cold War with the Soviets was the U.S.' primary concern. Like it or not, the United States was in bed with the Franco government.

And here was El Caudillo himself approaching. I knew I couldn't bring myself to shake hands with him as all the other diplomats were doing, embassy duty or not. But how could I escape doing so? If I created an incident by refusing to shake hands with Franco I would be on the first plane out of Spain within an hour on the insistence of the Spanish government. But first, I would get chewed out back at the embassy and this would surely mean the end of my diplomatic career. My annual fitness report would be a disaster. I would be encouraged, if not forced, to resign.

Franco was getting closer. There was no escaping him. What was I going to do? It was the ultimate damned if you do, damned if you don't situation. I may not have wanted to shake hands with Franco, but the United States had shaken both his hands and continued to do so on a daily basis.

I thought that if I moved a bit back perhaps Franco would go by without noticing me. Leaning back, I discovered immediately behind me a freestanding panel covered with pictures. Perhaps I could get behind it. I had to do something: Franco was only six diplomats away. Slowly, I backed up behind the screen and stood there hoping no one had noticed my disappearance. I imagined Franco must have been up to the Guatemalan ambassador. Now the African. Then, as I looked to my left I saw that he had already moved on down the row, was past where I had been. I waited another minute or so and then glided out from behind the temporary wall to take my place between the two ambassadors. Whether they had noticed my absence or not, they didn't say. My hunch is that they were so intent on their handshake and words with Franco that they hadn't missed me at all.

I had, presumably, escaped the Spanish government's wrath, but there might still be my own government to contend with. I was in mortal fear that someone would phone the United States Embassy to register a complaint. When I got to work the next day there would be hell to pay.

But when I did arrive no one said anything, and my brief report on attending the Spanish National Art Show, which traveled up through the hierarchy, was never questioned. Obviously, I did not mention how I had avoided shaking hands with Franco, though I was proud of having managed it. Perhaps if I had wanted to—though I decidedly did not—I could have been recruited some day by the C.I.A. I did seem to have secret agent potential.

# Hemingway, Bulls, and Me

ANY AMERICAN, ESPECIALLY ONE who fancied himself a writer and admired such books as *The Sun Also Rises* and *Death in the Afternoon,* would have had to be thinking some about Ernest Hemingway and bullfighting upon arriving in Spain not long after Hemingway's death. This was especially true of me because I had recently learned, checking dates, that when I had been examined at an American hospital in the spring of 1961, Ernest Hemingway was there as a patient under an assumed name.

I had gone there to be looked over by a team of psychiatrists prior to admission into the United States Diplomatic Service. I had passed the written test, the oral test, and the physical test. This was the next step: the mental health test. Obviously, the State Department didn't want any crazy people in the diplomatic service. I would learn that an occasional one slipped through the net, though a smaller percentage than one finds in universities.

The hospital I went to was the original Mayo Brothers Clinic in Rochester, Minnesota. It was only seventy-five miles from where I was doing my graduate work at the University of Minnesota. I stayed in a small bed and breakfast and went to the hospital two days in a row. I remember the psychiatrists showing me a lot of ink blots, the Rorschach test, which I had always considered ridiculous and still do. The ink blots all looked like butterflies to me, but I said that certain ones made me think of murdering my father, marrying my mother, and poking my eyes out. Of course, the shrinks immediately pronounced me admirably sane and cleared me for entering the government.

Hemingway was in that hospital shortly before he killed himself. Flying back home a few days after I had been in Rochester, he tried to jump out of a small, chartered plane. Early on the morning of July 2, 1961, he put a shotgun in his mouth at his home in Ketchum, Idaho and blew his head off.

In Spain, I felt as if I was accompanied by Hemingway's ghost. First, there was my deep admiration for his writing, especially that which dealt with Spain. But, also, many people I met in those days had known Hemingway and "knew" why he killed himself. A Spanish novelist friend told me that he had felt old, useless, and had become sexually impotent. A professor at the University of Madrid authoritatively said that he killed himself because he had skin cancer on his face and that his beard was an attempt to cover it.

The most interesting theory was that of a female American bullfighter. I had been invited to dinner by a number of American and Spanish friends at the tiny El Callejon Restaurant in downtown Madrid. This, I was told, was Hemingway's favorite restaurant in Madrid. He had written and drawn all over the walls with a pencil, and it was fun to walk around and examine his comments and doodles. Unfortunately, this restaurant no longer exists. If it did, it would be a shrine for Hemingway fans around the world. At the very least, those scribbles on the wall should have been preserved somehow, perhaps not unlike how Goya's frescos from his black period were removed from the walls of his home, known as La Quinta del Sordo, and transported to the Prado Museum.

The lady bullfighter was placed next to me at the table. I did not know that there occasionally were female bullfighters. I didn't even know then about rejoneadores (those who fight bulls on horseback and do not kill them), though this woman insisted she was a regular torero and told me so. Whether she had been or not, she lifted her shirt and showed me her abdomen, which was crisscrossed by several horrible scars. Her belly looked like it had been clumsily sewn together by a shoemaker using large leather stitches.

She claimed to have been part of Hemingway's entourage during his last summer in Spain in 1959 and said that he was obviously in love with a bullfighter. She implied that, unable to tolerate these homosexual longings, he had killed himself. Hemingway's book, *The Dangerous Summer* is about the *mano a mano* (one on one), three bulls each instead of the customary two, between Antonio Ordóñez and Luis Miguel Dominguín, as they traveled about Spain with their cuadrillas (their team of banderilleros and picadors) from one bull ring to another. I don't recall which torero the lady bullfighter said Hemingway had been

The author and his wife in the bull ring of Ronda, Hemingway's favorite.

in love with, but, in the book, he obviously admires Ordóñez considerably more than Dominguín.

Was there truth in what she said? Certainly, Hemingway's super macho behavior and attitudes—regularly challenging other men to box, constantly presenting himself in hyper-masculine terms, four wives and a multitude of affairs—might suggest a need to squelch feelings of a different sort. His unfinished novel, published posthumously, *The Garden of Eden*, replete as it is with all sorts of gender uncertainty, does suggest a side of Hemingway entirely unlike his chest thumping public persona. And his need to put men down for not being "sufficiently manly" according to his criteria—the character Robert Cohn in *The Sun Also Rises,* F. Scott Fitzgerald in the memoir, *A Moveable Feast*—suggests a man uncertain of his masculinity, a man who felt he had something to prove.

Frankly, though these stories may each have had some validity to them, and helped precipitate Hemingway's mental illness, I don't think they caused him to kill himself. He killed himself because he was deeply depressed at a time when depression was ill-understood and anti-depressants were in their infancy. Also, suicide ran in his family, beginning with his father and ending with his granddaughter, the beautiful actress and model, Margaux Hemingway. Throughout his life, Hemingway would refer to periods of what he called "blackass," which was his word for depression. In 1961 he was, no doubt, suffering his most serious case of "blackass" yet, and it led to his hospitalization. His spirits were so low as to make him non-functional, and he foresaw no remedy for it.

Whatever the true reasons for Hemingway's suicide, it affected me more than most. Like other young writers, I had yearned for a dramatic and romantic life like Hemingway's and dreamed of literary distinction like his. In those days he stood alone among American writers for me. There was Hemingway and then there were the others. Norman Mailer referred to Hemingway as "the champ." No other American writer, with the possible exception of Mark Twain, has had such an influence on American writing—the short sentences, the use of few adjectives, the clean, unencumbered prose. As with Twain, Hemingway's writing is vernacular, rejects European influences and American writers such as Henry James and T. S. Eliot, who aspired to European complexities. Along with Twain, Hemingway was the key writer to demonstrate that Ralph Waldo Emerson's hope for a native literature had been fulfilled.

But since Hemingway's life ended in suicide, perhaps the man I imagined and wished to emulate was something of a myth. Nevertheless, I was now in Spain, and nothing had made me love Spain even before I got there as did Hemingway's writing. And the bullfight was central to his vision of Spain and of a life fully lived.

So, upon arrival in Spain I began to go regularly to the bullfights. There were two active bullrings in Madrid, Las Ventas and Vista Alegre, and a third bullring just outside the city in the town of San Sebastian de los Reyes, where they had only novillos (young, smaller bulls), but it was easier to get last minute tickets. Most Sundays during the season I went to one of these three bullrings. I delighted in the pageantry of the bull fight, the colorful costumes, the cries of "Musica!" followed by a stirring *pasadoble*, the magnificent animals, the danger, the very sand of the arena. I have never enjoyed drinking wine as much as when sprayed into my mouth from a bota (a leather wine skin) on a hot afternoon. Sure, bullfighting was barbaric, sure it involved considerable cruelty to animals. But that was what my head told me. My heart was another matter.

I even tried my own skill at bullfighting when invited by Spanish friends to what is called a *tienta* at a ranch outside Madrid. I was given a red rag and climbed into the ring with other amateurs. There were several animals running about at once. These were not bulls we were "fighting"; they weren't even *novillos*. They were calves, and the little horns of those who had already sprouted them were padded. Surely I could handle these animals I told myself.

"*Toro,*" I yelled, though these calves were hardly bulls; they were not dramatically larger than Saint Bernards. One now saw me and charged. I bravely held my ground, curved my body as I had seen so many *toreros* (bullfighters) do, the red rag fluttering in my right hand, invitingly. Despite my efforts with it, the calf was still coming, straight for me. I was frightened, but I stood my ground. Surely he would veer off at the last moment, attracted by my skills with the rag.

He didn't. The red rag meant nothing to that calf. He (and I'm not entirely certain it *was* a "he") hit me solidly and sent me flying over his back and through the air some twenty-five feet. I landed, more embarrassed than hurt, especially with all of the laughter coming from friends and other spectators. It continued after I scurried into the stands. A friend consoled me: "Excellent," he said, "not quite the equal of El Cordobes, but excellent." This was the period when El Cordobes, with his great daring and showmanship, was the dominant figure in Spanish bullfighting

I shall never understand how I did not break several bones that day, though I did wake up the next morning so stiff I needed help getting out of bed. I hurt in many places and was black and blue for several weeks afterwards. I also paid several visits to a chiropractor who said my body needed to be "realigned." I thought it needed to be replaced rather than realigned.

This incident should have convinced me that I had no talent for bullfighting. Nevertheless, the next year found me at the San Fermines in Pamplona. With several days vacation from the embassy I ran with the big bulls, averaging 550 kilos, each morning through the streets of that fabled town. Well, I didn't exactly run *with* the bulls. I stayed so far ahead of them that I never saw them until after I had made it into the ring and up into the stands.

I'd prefer to believe that I was wise rather than a coward. I could not have handled anything more challenging given how much wine I drank each night and how exhausted I was by morning. As was the custom, I stayed up all night drinking and dancing in the streets, my arms around strangers who, no doubt because of the wine, seemed like the best friends I'd ever had. Shortly after sunup, there would be the running of the bulls from the corral at the other end of town, down a main street that was blocked off at its intersections, until the *enciero* (sequestration) at the corral of the bull ring. Then I would retire to an old Spanish lady's home where I had managed to rent not a room but a narrow cot at a ruinous price. Despite all the others in the room, I slept soundly most of the day and awakened in time for the bullfight in the late afternoon. Then it started all over again.

During the hours of drinking and dancing each night I often found myself expecting to encounter Ernest Hemingway or Jake or Lady Brett or some of the other characters from *The Sun Also Rises*. Actually, there *was* someone I did recognize each evening. It was the American consul from Bilbao, our closest post to Pamplona. He looked entirely out of place. Standing in a doorway in the shadows, he wore a suit and tie and dress shoes, no doubt the only one of any nationality dressed in this fashion during the days of the San Fermines. He was apparently on duty to attend to any Americans who got into a drunken fight or got gored or even got killed.

A Spanish fellow next to me asked, "Who is that man?"

"I haven't the slightest idea," I responded. The last thing I wanted was to be identified just then with the embassy by my fellow, drunken dancers, with whom I snaked through the streets in an interminably long line. I felt as if I had been born for the San Fermines!

One evening the Bilbao consul approached, took me by the arm, separated me from the other dancers, and steered me into the dark doorway. "I'm not going to have any trouble with you, Michael, am I?" he asked rhetorically. Clearly, if an American diplomat got into difficulties during the San Fermines that would have been more serious than a Spaniard or even an American tourist getting into trouble. A diplomat getting into trouble during the fiesta might have constituted an international incident.

"No problem, Herbert," I said, adding, "Why don't you lighten up? Get out of these clothes and have some wine."

"I can't," he said, "I'm on duty."

"I won't tell," I replied. "But if you're determined to spy on all the Americans, including me, you'd be much more effective if you fit in. You look like an absolute stiff standing over here in the dark." I ran to rejoin the dancers, but Herbert's presence put a bit of a crimp in my enjoyment of the festival.

After my years with the embassy I would increasingly hear that bullfighting was becoming of less interest in Spain and even controversial. First, soccer continued to gain in popularity. But it also seemed that bullfighting, like flamenco, was seen by young Spaniards as representing a traditional Spain from which they wished to separate themselves. In addition, animal rights activists were increasingly attacking bullfighting.

Recently there was word that the Catalans were thinking of banning bullfighting altogether. *The New York Times* had a story in October 2009 titled "In a Spanish Province, the Twilight of the Matadors." According to the *Times,* "Catalan nationalists...spread the notion that *toreo* [bullfighting] was an imposition on Catalonia by Franco's fascist regime, which promoted it, like flamenco, as a patriotic symbol." Far be it from me to defend anything associated with Francisco Franco, but if a foreigner may be so bold: I think those people were mistaken. Catalonia was the very center of bullfighting in Spain for many years before

Franco's dictatorship. Also, as Paco March, bullfighting writer from *La Vanguardia,* is quoted as saying in the same *Times* article, "We want to be different from the rest of Spain by not killing bulls, but we're just killing off our own culture." He might have added that Catalanes in the South of France also wish to distinguish themselves from the other French, and they do so through their passion for bullfighting, which is banned in Paris. In a July, 2010 *New York Times* article I read to my consternation that the Catalan parliament had indeed banned bullfighting throughout Catalonia beginning in January of 2012.

This is sad. Must Spain be like the rest of Europe or might it maintain traditions of its own? I do hope Catalonia's example is not followed elsewhere in Spain—though bullfighting had earlier been banned in Spain's two provinces in the Canary Islands. For me, getting rid of bullfighting would be evidence of Spain McDonaldizing itself. It will be entirely too bad if a day arrives when those reading *The Sun Also Rises* experience something quaint, long gone, or even of no particular meaning to them, who would not crave, as I did, the romance and foolhardiness of "fighting" a calf at a *tienta* or running with— even if well ahead of— the bulls in Pamplona. There is already too much homogenizing of cultures around the world. Is it in anyone's interest that Spain become just another European country? Those of us who admire it do so precisely because it isn't just another European country.

One of the things I like best about Spain is that pagan characteristics are still in evidence, whereas they have been all but obliterated elsewhere in Europe. And pagans get a bad rap. One thing the pagans knew how to do was to enjoy themselves. Even their gods weren't a somber lot. They had a grand time rolling about in heaven, drinking wine and having sex. Good for them!

In shedding bullfighting Spain would be losing one of its most important pagan antecedents, and that would be too bad. I've often wondered whether bullfighting might account for Spaniards being less bellicose, less warlike than Americans. They argue, they call each other unspeakable names, but they rarely hit one another, don't shoot each other, and they usually stay out of wars. Could one reason for this be because they satisfy their taste for blood in the bullring, that bullfighting is a remnant of the ancient practice of animal sacrifice? Isn't that what Abraham, and perhaps God, had in mind when Abraham desisted from killing his own son, Isaac and killed a ram instead? I like animals as much as the next person, but my first allegiance is to my own species. Anything that might make human beings less murderous towards each other sounds pretty good to me. And perhaps bullfighting is one of those things.

Barbaric and cruel it may be, but bullfighting could also represent a higher civilization. Perhaps we Americans should take up bullfighting. It might do us a lot of good. Would bullfighting Americans have been so bellicose and stupid as to invade Iraq? I doubt it.

# With Martin Luther King in Madrid

SEPTEMBER 19, 1964 already felt like it would be a hot day when my office phone rang early that morning in Madrid. It was Ambassador Woodward. Was I in trouble? He had never before called me directly, and, as a very junior Embassy functionary, and having been in Madrid less than nine months, I was apprehensive.

The Ambassador told me he had just received a cable from the American Embassy in Rome saying that Martin Luther King was en route to Madrid and would be staying for a day prior to flying to Amsterdam to keynote an international Baptist convention. I had already had news of King that day. The Spanish newspaper, *ABC*, which I had perused over breakfast, had a full, front page picture of him in audience with Pope Paul VI in Rome the day before.

The ambassador asked me to look after King while he was in Madrid. I guessed this was attributable to my having once casually mentioned to him at a cocktail party that I had written a major paper for my Masters Degree on the Montgomery Bus Boycott of 1956, which first brought King to world attention. I was thrilled to have the King assignment. The previous year he had made his "I Have a Dream" speech at the August 28,

1963 March on Washington, one of the greatest piece of oratory in American history. There were rumors in the press that he might soon be awarded the Nobel Peace Prize, which actually did happen shortly after I was with him. The Ambassador gave me King's flight number and told me I could have the official limousine and chauffeur to go to Barajas Airport to fetch him.

Phoning the airport, I learned that King's plane had landed an hour before; there was no way I could pick him up. More important, I had no idea where in the vast city of Madrid he might be staying. The cable from Rome had said nothing about it. I didn't even know for sure he was staying at a hotel, but I got out the telephone directory and began calling hotels, one after another. It was a little like looking for the proverbial needle in a haystack, but I had to find King. The Embassy was already receiving nonstop telephone calls inquiring as to his whereabouts and demanding interviews. I needed to shield King from unwanted attention, but I couldn't do this unless I found him before the media did.

The last place I anticipated finding him was the Castellana Hilton (now the Castellana Intercontinental) just across Madrid's main thoroughfare from the back of the embassy and the closest hotel. I hadn't thought he could be there because that would have been too easy. But on what must have been my twentieth hotel telephone call I had the following conversation with the Hilton's desk clerk:

"Has a Dr. King checked into your hotel in the last hour or so?"

"No, there's no *king* staying here. We once had a duke and a marquis, but never a king."

"He's not *a* king. His *name* is King."

The desk clerk consulted his registry. He said, "A black guy with the name 'Kingo' checked in a little while ago. A doctor? He didn't say anything about being a doctor. I don't think we ever had a black guy stay here before...." He probably would have continued in this chatty vein, but I had already replaced the receiver and was running out the Embassy door.

Dodging traffic, I crossed the Castellana and entered the lobby of the hotel. I picked up a phone and asked to be connected to King's room.

A tired voice said "Hello."

" Dr. King?"

"Yes."

"This is Michael Rockland," I said rapidly. "I'm with the Embassy and have been assigned to look after you while you're in Madrid. If it's convenient, I'd like to come up to your room to inform you about things you may want to do in Madrid. There's also the media to be concerned about. In any case, I'm completely at your service."

For what seemed an interminable time: silence. Then the same tired voice said, "I'm sorry, but I don't speak Spanish."

"What?" I asked incredulously.

"I don't speak Spanish," he repeated.

"But I'm not speaking Spanish," I exclaimed. Ava Gardner thought I spoke English well for a Spaniard. King thought I was speaking Spanish instead of

English. I delivered my short speech again, this time more slowly.

King was apparently exhausted from his travels, the time zone changes, and from the altitude and heat of Madrid. And, of course, there was the language barrier. Resigned to not being able to communicate with anyone while in Madrid, he had mistaken my quick, New York accented English, so different from the laconic speech of southerners, for more of the Spanish whose meaning had been eluding him. But now he said, sounding almost grateful, "Oh, yes, please come up."

When I knocked on the door of room 209, Martin Luther King answered dressed in his white boxer shorts. His single bed was rumpled. He had obviously been napping. It was hot in his room; in those days there was little air conditioning in Spanish hotels.

Here was a revered and famous figure, in the news almost daily, and he was receiving me clothed in nothing but underpants. American informality on full parade.

It also exhibited itself in his insisting I call him Martin, so we were "Michael" and "Martin" right from the start. It felt a little strange addressing him by his first name. It was as if I had lived in the mid-nineteenth century and been invited to address Abraham Lincoln as "Abe."

King said he'd never been to Spain before and hoped to just relax and "see the sights" before going to Holland the next day. Would I mind accompanying him?

Would I?! I could not have thought of anything I preferred to do. But I warned King that the media was searching all over Madrid and would soon be harassing him. I suggested we schedule a single press conference of half an hour and refuse all other requests. Somewhat reluctantly, he agreed, so I phoned the press attaché at the embassy and asked him to set it up for an hour from then in one of the hotel conference rooms. Might as well get it over with.

I then asked Martin if he had any pressing needs. He hesitated but finally admitted that he had "a terrible case of diarrhea" that had started in Rome. I was surprised that Martin Luther King suffered from the same maladies as other human beings. "I'll be right back," I said. I ran to a nearby pharmacy, purchased an over-the-counter remedy well-known to me, and had it back to King in ten minutes. History will record that I am the man who personally cured Martin Luther King's diarrhea in Madrid, Spain on September 19, 1964. I won't object if a plaque is some day fastened outside room 209 of that hotel to mark the event.

After Martin had taken two of the pills the phone rang. He answered it and then said, smiling, "You'd better handle it. This person is *definitely* not speaking English."

"I am a Protestant minister," the caller began. "I wish to greet Dr. King." Apparently this minister planned to attend the upcoming Baptist gathering in Amsterdam and had found out from someone there where King was staying in Madrid. I asked Martin if the minister could come up and meet him.

Exhausted, he asked if it was necessary. I told him about the tough situation of all non-Catholics in Spain in those days, Protestants perhaps even more so than Jews or Muslims. Protestants weren't just an underground culture; for them, the Counter-reformation was still underway. In the United States then Protestants were the establishment, but in Spain they were "the enemy." Indeed, I imagined that King's own name, "Martin Luther," would not in those days be treated as an entirely casual fact in Spain. I told Martin that if he received the minister (briefly, I promised) he would be doing a kindly and important deed.

A few moments later there was a knock and the minister stood stiffly in the doorway. The scene must have amazed him. There, just behind me, was Martin Luther King—who the minister had often seen in the media being threatened by dogs, jailed, singing "We Shall Overcome"; who had appeared in that morning's Madrid newspapers with the pope—and here he was standing in his boxers to greet this entirely buttoned up, carefully dressed Spanish minister who kept staring at King, apparently unsure what to do. But overcoming inhibitions, he rushed past me to throw his arms around Martin's gleaming, sweating body in a *fuerte abrazo* (a big hug).

I shall never forget the expression on Martin Luther King's face as he looked at me over the minister's shoulder, his eyes fairly popping out of his head. He seemed to be imploring me to explain what he was supposed to do about an overly affectionate Spaniard. Americans were not familiar with males hugging in those days. Of course, our current president, Barack Obama, hugs everyone.

Mercifully, the minister soon released King and told him (I translated) what "an inspiration you are for us here in Spain. The struggle of the Negroes for freedom and respect in the United States is not unlike our struggle in Spain, where we can only practice our religion in secrecy. God bless you."

Martin blessed the minister in return and I quickly escorted him to the door. There was only half an hour till the press conference. Martin took a shower and I turned on the television, which, in those days, if I recall correctly, consisted of only a single state/ church channel that went off the air at around 10 p.m. I wondered whether word of Martin's arrival in Madrid was being broadcast and, sure enough, the news carried the photograph of Martin and the pope and information on our upcoming press conference. There was even live coverage of the preparations downstairs in the hotel for the upcoming press conference.

King and I descended in the elevator and entered a large room on the ground floor that was already crowded with some fifty print and broadcast journalists. Everyone seemed to be pushing and shoving, the embassy press attaché trying to maintain order. Martin and I stepped before two microphones, bright lights almost blinding us. There were a series of questions, most fairly inane:

"Dr. King. What impression did the pope make on you?"

Ambassador Robert Woodward who gave the author the Martin Luther King assignment, with some promising, democratically oriented students the author had recruited for fellowships in the United States, the author himself on the right.

"Dr. King. How do you like Spain?" King didn't know what to say to this. All he'd seen of Spain thus far was a taxi, a small room, and a passionate Protestant minister. He whispered to me, "What do I say?" I told him not to worry about it and told the media, as if translating his whisper, that he was very much enjoying Spain and the great Spanish people. I was, after all, a diplomat.

"Dr. King, how long will you be staying in Spain?"

"Dr. King, where will you be traveling when you leave Spain?"

"Dr. King, doesn't it seem to you that things are much more tranquil here in Spain than in the United States?" Again, Martin whispered in my ear, "What do

I say?" I knew that the thing to say—making Spaniards happy while not running down the United States— was that some things were more tranquil in Spain and other things were more tranquil in the United States. "Tell them, please," Martin said, and I did.

There were a few more, equally inconsequential questions and we had reached the agreed upon half hour mark. The press conference was called to a halt and Martin and I escaped into the lobby. Martin was so exhausted now that he stumbled as he crossed the threshold of his room. I urged him to take a nap, and he said he would. We agreed that I would return in three hours. Before departing, I called the hotel front desk and told them, "No telephone calls. I don't care if it's Francisco Franco or Lyndon Johnson."

I returned at 2 p.m., normal lunchtime for any-one used to Spanish gastronomic ways, but Martin was already up, dressed, and starving. The ambas-sador's limousine and chauffeur were waiting for us downstairs, and we rode in style down to Restaurante Botin on the Calle Cuchilleros, just beyond the Plaza Mayor. I knew Botin's was where all the tourists have gone ever since Hemingway placed there the final scene in *The Sun Also Rises*, but, after all, Martin *was* a tourist just then. There was a table for two avail-able in the bodega below street level. I suggested the famous sopa al cuarto de hora (fifteen minute soup) and the cordero asado (roast lamb) for us both, and Martin readily agreed.

There were other Americans down in the bo-dega. In those days any black person in Madrid was a novelty, but one who looked just like Martin Luther King? People at other tables stared at us. I overheard a man at a nearby table say to his wife, "No, that's not him. Just looks like him." I wasn't about to tell him otherwise.

While we waited for our food we finally had a chance to talk. I asked Martin if he knew of the murder in the South of two civil rights workers that had taken place the day before. Since he had been traveling, he might not have heard of this tragedy. He did know.

"Damned South," I said. In those days, if you were a northern liberal, you generally thought of the South, however unfairly, as the epicenter of American racism and of everything else that was wrong with the United States. This conveniently let the North off the hook

King looked at me curiously. "But *I'm* a Southerner," he said.

"Yes," I said—and I shall always be embarrassed by what I said next—"but you aren't a *real* Southerner." What I meant was that, since he was the most prominent black leader of the day, he couldn't be a real Southerner because I equated Southerners with evil.

"No," Martin said, "I *am* a real Southerner."

Now it was my turn to look at Martin curiously. I asked him how he could think of himself that way.

"It's simply who I am," he said. "It's my history."

"Yes," I said, "but why identify yourself with a history of three hundred years of slavery and one hundred years of segregation and Jim Crow and lynching?"

"A person's history is their history, good or bad," he said. And then, knowing I am a Jew, he said, "What's so great about your history, Michael? The modern history of Jews is far worse than the modern history of black people. Is that history something with which you don't identify, that you want to forget?"

"No," I said, "I'd cut off my hand before I forgot the murder of six million of my people, two out of five of all of us on the planet. I live my life dedicated to their memory, never forget them for a minute."

"Then why," Martin asked, "do you want me to forget my people's history?"

He was right, of course, but I still didn't like the way the conversation was going. It's hard when your hero is not in full agreement with you. I was a universalist in those days. I imagined that one day race and religion and ethnicity and national origin would all be lost in the greater humanity. Though proud of my own heritage, I believed in the melting pot. I had not yet sought out an alternate metaphor for explaining the United States such as the salad bowl or the mosaic. Multiculturalism was not yet on the horizon for me. But it clearly was already part of Martin's thinking.

When I told him that I didn't know how we would ever get rid of racism in America until we got rid of races—all of us intermarrying until we might have a post racial society—Martin said that he hoped for no such thing. "I want to get rid of racism," he said, "but not races. God is a pluralist. Wouldn't the world be a dull place without such variety?" Again, in my youthful idealism, I felt a certain disquiet. When we admire someone as much as I admired him, we want them to agree with us. It makes it easier to keep agreeing with them.

After lunch Martin said he wanted to go shopping for gifts for his family. It was 4:00 p.m.; the stores, closed for the midday meal and siesta, would be reopening. The Embassy limousine carried us to a shop I knew just off the Plaza de Canovas and double parked, the diplomatic corps plates providing cover. I failed to interest Martin in what I considered the better things: gorgeous ceramics from Talavera, Toledo ware. He wanted bullfight posters with his son's names on them and little bulls and bullfighters. He wanted flamenco dolls for his daughters. I restrained myself from saying anything. Of course, those were the things he wanted. He had never been to Spain before. I had to keep reminding myself that, in this instance, Martin Luther King was like any other tourist. Nevertheless, there was a lesson I learned over and over that day: great men can also be ordinary in many ways.

Martin also bought a black lace mantilla for his wife. I wondered whether Coretta Scott King ever wore the mantilla. When Martin was killed there were pictures of Coretta in the newspapers wearing a veil at his funeral that looked a lot like the mantilla he had purchased that day.

We deposited Martin's "loot" in the Embassy car, and I told the chauffeur to drop off the gifts at the hotel and then be available to take the ambassador home. I figured Martin and I could take a cab back to his hotel later or walk. Besides, Martin said what he needed most was some fresh air and exercise.

We spent the rest of the afternoon walking in Retiro Park, where Martin revealed an ordinary side to him that was a bit too much for me to tolerate. I've always loved geography, and I don't think I've ever met anyone less schooled in it than Martin Luther King. We had stopped at a café in the park and ordered coffees. In those days, before the American coffee revolution, you couldn't get a decent cup of coffee in the United States, and Martin kept talking about how good the Spanish coffee was and ordered a second cup. Then he asked me a series of startlingly naïve geographical questions.

"Tell me," he said, "We're here in Madrid, right? Okay, in which direction is Rome from here?" At first I thought he must be joking, but I took a napkin and drew with a ballpoint pen the square outlines of the Iberian Peninsula and the boot of Italy, placing dots on the map for Madrid and Rome. "It's more or less East," I said.

And Holland, where I'm going tomorrow? Where is it?"

I sketched in northern Europe and said, "More or less northeast."

Finally, he said: "And the United States? Where is it from here?" Now I thought he *really* had to be kidding me. Could he possibly not know in which direction the United States was from Spain? But he was serious. On the napkin I sketched the East Coast of the United States— with prominent features such as Maine and Florida sticking out—and between it and the Iberian Peninsula I put some waves. "That's the Atlantic I said."

Here was a guy about to receive the Nobel Prize and he didn't know where anything was. Well, I would remind myself in later years, in elementary school, Einstein was lousy at math.

Later we had a light supper at the counter of one of Madrid's innumerable Museos del Jamon. Then, as the sun disappeared, we walked the mile or so up the Castellana to the Hilton. I made arrangements to pick him up the next morning to take him to the airport.

At Barajas, I got out of the embassy limousine with Martin to help him with his suitcase, and he did something which was new to him—no doubt learned from the Protestant minister the previous day. He put his arms around me and gave me an abrazo. That hug meant a great deal to me. I can almost feel it still. It's really all I have of my time with Martin in Madrid. I never saw him again.

I do wish I had kept the napkin I had drawn on in Retiro Park. I've mentioned it to my students at Rutgers University, but they've never been interested. What they always want to know is why I never got a picture taken of myself with Martin that he inscribed to me. "You were with a real celebrity," they say, "how come you didn't get a picture." I don't think there's a word I dislike more than the word "celebrity." And, besides, the charm of my time with Martin Luther King in Madrid was precisely that we were just Martin and Michael. It wasn't about being with "a celebrity." Had I gotten someone to take a picture of us together and gotten him to sign it, it would have put a certain distance between us, spoiled what was special about being with him on an even footing—just two men walking around Madrid together.

These days there are pictures of Martin in almost every public school classroom in the United States and a monumental statue in Washington, D.C. A national holiday has been created in his honor. He certainly merits these things but, at the same time, I hate that we've turned him into something unreal— something sterile, plastic. The man I knew was certainly a hero, but he had his faults. And when he was killed, I wept as much for his lost faults as for his lost greatness.

I have always had the good fortune to be able to weep for Martin not as a saint but as a man—a man who had something so basic as diarrhea when I met him. Also, despite his worldwide fame, he had never fully outgrown his origins as a Southern Baptist preacher. And, yet, he was also a genius, for want of a better word, at what he did best.

# A Jew in Spain

IN THE BAR OF A SMALL Spanish village in Asturias, a region in northern Spain, I had become an object of curiosity. The men were kindly teaching an American how to pour the wonderful hard cider of the region. I struggled to hold the bottle properly over my head in my right hand, the wide mouthed glass tipped outward in my left hand by my left hip so that, when the cider hit the outer rim, it would bounce in and foam up. The sawdust on the floor and the left side of my trousers were completely soaked, but I, like the others, was pretty drunk by this time so it didn't matter. Being drunk may have been what emboldened my friends to ask if I was Catholic or atheist. These seemed to be the only choices readily familiar to them.

"Neither," I said.

One of them looked at me speculatively. "Protestant?" he asked.

"No," I said, "Jewish." This astounded them. It was as if I had announced that I was a Martian. None of them had ever met a Jew before. Jews seemed to be legendary creatures they had heard of but weren't sure still existed. Also, they seemed surprised that one could be both an American diplomat and Jewish. The one who had asked if I was Protestant said, "I thought everyone in the American government was a

Michelangelo's *Moses* in the San Pietro in Vincoli church in Rome. Please note the horns.

Protestant." I reminded them about Kennedy having been Catholic.

But something more important was on their minds than my religion per se. "Where are your horns?" one man asked. Another ruffled my hair—gingerly, as if fearing some contagion—and reported to the others: "No horns at all." Then he asked me, "Are you sure you're Jewish?"

This superstition about Jews having horns stems from a mistranslation of the Hebrew Bible (we don't call it "The Old Testament" because, for us, there is no "New"). Moses is described as having rays of light shining down on his head from heaven. One of my children, actually born in Madrid, is named Keren, which, in Hebrew, means "ray of light." Those rays became "horns of light" in the Vulgate or Catholic version of the Hebrew Bible, but even "horns of light" would not imply "horns." In Rome, there is, in the parish church of San Pietro in Vincoli, a Michelangelo marble statue depicting Moses with horns. When I saw it, I didn't know whether to be offended or to laugh—maybe both.

Whatever my general disappointment with the Christian world, I had, when I first arrived at the American Embassy in Madrid, an extra chip on my shoulder as regards Spain. I recalled the photograph of Franco cordially greeting Hitler at Hendaye— though it could be said that by keeping Hitler at bay and out of Spain, Franco, even if unintentionally, kept open an escape avenue for some Jews fleeing the Holocaust and also precluded Hitler from marching across Spain to attack British Gibraltar, so crucial to the eventual allied victory through its control of the entrance of the Mediterranean. I also knew about the Spanish Blue Division which fought alongside the Nazis in Russia. Most important, Spain was the country that had once given my people three choices: leave, convert, or be burned at the stake. Not as bad as the Nazis, but none too friendly.

Some Spanish friends would say to me, "Well, at least the Inquisition was not racist." This may be true, but it could hardly have mattered to someone being burned at the stake whether this was because of his race or his religion. Jews are, almost uniquely, both a people and a religion, so enemies over the centuries have had two avenues of persecution, which is, perhaps, one reason for our being such an easy target.

Whether fair or not, for Americans today, Catholics along with everyone else, the term "The Spanish Inquisition" is almost a redundancy; Spain and the Inquisition are intimately linked in the American mind. Americans have also had difficulty understanding why Ferdinand and Isabel are celebrated in Spain. They may have been The Catholic Kings, but they were hardly Christians—if by "Christian" one means those who seek to emulate the wisdom and behavior of Jesus. They also mutilated Spain by getting rid of two of the three cultures that made the country great, including the majority of its poets and scientists. Spain became a secondary country, a status from which it would take centuries to recover.

Many Jews followed Muslim co-exiles into the Arab lands where, for centuries, they were treated far better than they had been in Christian Europe. Of course, when Israel was reestablished by the United Nations in 1947, and declared its independence in 1948, the Sephardic Jews fled the ensuing persecution of the Arabs, the great majority going to Israel. More than half the Israeli Jewish population consists of these folks, whose primary native tongue and culture was Arabic. People mistakenly assume that Arabs are all Muslims, but just as there are Christian Arabs, there are, in effect, Jewish ones as well. In addition, the Sephardics have always spoken Ladino (medieval Spanish) at home, writing it in Hebrew letters, as Yiddish (medieval German) also utilizes Hebrew letters. In various professional trips to Israel I have used my Spanish regularly in conversation with these Ladino-speaking Sephardics. It is similar, I should think, to what it would be like returning to an earlier England and having a conversation with Shakespeare or Chaucer in which I would speak modern English and they Elizabethan or Middle English. Many of the Sephardics I would meet did not speak English because their primary concern, integrating themselves into Israeli society, required learning Hebrew.

For Jews, Hebrew had long been only a liturgical language, a language of prayer, much as Latin had been for Catholics. To this day there are ultra-Orthodox Jews who rage against Israel for making "the language of God" the language of the streets. Hebrew, for them, may only become an everyday language when the Messiah arrives. They consider its use in Israel today as blasphemous. My own view is that every group, including my own, has its crazy people.

Despite the fact that Judaism was essentially expunged from Spain by the Inquisition and centuries of persecution, many Spaniards, learning I am Jewish, immediately insist that they are part Jewish. From a Jewish point of view, one is Jewish or not; you can't be Catholic or something else and claim to be "part-Jewish." Jews may be a people but they're not a race. Also, the physical characteristics of Jews have changed so markedly over the centuries, mostly through the wholesale rape of Jewish women (which is why Judaism is matrilineal) and intermarriage, that the word "anti-Semitism" badly needs reconsideration. Except for the Sephardics in Israel, who are largely indistinguishable in appearance from Arabs, Jews, especially those from a European background, don't, for the most part, look Semitic. There are, for example, a fair number of blond, blue eyed Jews. So many members of my Reform Jewish synagogue in New Jersey are in, or the product of, mixed marriages that we often joke, "What's the matter with this congregation? Nobody looks Jewish." Ironically, it is for the most part the Arabs who are the Semites today. Anti-Semitism should be a word referring to those who hate Arabs. A new word must be found for people who hate us.

I suspect Jesus looked very Semitic, which underscores the idiocy, if not outright Aryan racism, of Hollywood films that pick blond, blue eyed actors— Tab Hunter, Max von Sydow, Willem Dafoe to name three—to play Jesus in movies. The only good thing one might say about Mel Gibson's patently anti-Semitic story of Jesus, *The Passion of the Christ* (2004) is that at least his Jesus was dark. In Salt Lake City the Mormons picture Jesus as being about 7 feet tall and with long, beautiful blond hair and piercing blue eyes. If Jesus had actually looked that way it would, in part, have explained his extraordinary appeal, since no one else in the Holy Land did. I think it more likely Jesus looked as the Italian film director, Pier Paulo Pasolini, portrayed him in his move *The Gospel*

*According to St. Matthew* (1964), in which the actor playing him appears short, dark, and disturbed.

The day after seeing this movie in Madrid I reported the fact to my embassy secretary, a lovely Spanish woman of Irish Argentine ancestry. "Evelina," I said, "you won't believe it: in Pasolini's movie Jesus' brothers and sisters appear."

Evelina, normally the sweetest woman on the planet, became enraged. I thought my reporting on the movie would be a neutral matter or might even be considered evidence of an ecumenical spirit, but Evelina said indignantly, "Jesus didn't have brothers and sisters. If he had, his mother wouldn't have been the Virgin Mary. There wouldn't have been The Immaculate Conception."

Already having three children by then, I was and am (with five children total now) more admiring of "maculate" conception myself; and I am worshipful of women's wondrous sexuality and assign no virtue to virginity. Nevertheless, I said, "couldn't Jesus' conception have been immaculate but his later siblings not? In Matthew, at least, his brothers and sisters—presumably born after him, and conceived by Mary and Joseph in the traditional way—are mentioned. They are also with Mary at the cross."

"Not in my bible!" Evelina said angrily, which, I learned, was actually true. The Catholic or Vulgate edition of the Christian bible has, indeed, gotten rid of those inconvenient siblings, while they are present in the King James, or Protestant, version. In any case, it took a full month before Evelina would speak to me again. I vowed never to discuss religion with her again. As the American television talk show host, Johnny Carson, once put it, "There are two things one cannot discuss with other people in a rational manner: pets and religion."

At one point in my years in Spain I experienced a contretemps over religion more serious than that with Evelina. Christmas was approaching and my boss sent me a note asking me to organize the Embassy Christmas party. This seemed a strange request. Why would I, then the only Jew in the embassy, be asked to organize the embassy Christmas party? Thinking there must be some mistake, I went to see him.

"I know you're Jewish," he said, "so I thought you would consider it an honor to organize the Embassy Christmas party."

I didn't know what to say. An *honor*? "But I don't celebrate Christmas," I told him.

"That's why I asked you," he said. "I wanted you to feel included."

Included? I had often joined Christian friends in celebrating their holidays, just as they had often joined me in celebrating mine, but I certainly never organized their religious occasions nor did I expect them to organize mine.

"Well," I said to my boss, "it's very kind of you, but I wouldn't feel comfortable doing that." I neglected to add that the whole idea of an official embassy Christmas party contradicts the American Constitution, which prohibits the favoring of any religion by the government and erects a high wall of separation between church and state. Parties at home or in religious or private institutions are fine; government parties or parties in public spaces are not. An embassy Christmas party was indeed, I thought, a joining of church and state.

But my boss wasn't going to let up. "Why are you so sensitive?" he asked. "Christmas isn't a religious holiday. It's just about Santa Claus and Christmas trees, and songs like "Rudolph the Red Nosed Reindeer" and "Jingle Bells."

"Really?" I asked, "I thought Christmas celebrates the birth of Jesus Christ." I was certainly in a strange position: a Jew arguing against the secularization of Christmas, actually trying, as a Spanish friend laughingly told me later, "to put Christ back into Christmas."

My boss was becoming angry. "You absolutely refuse to organize the embassy Christmas party?"

"I think someone else would be more appropriate," I replied.

We never spoke of this matter again, but I was left anxious and unhappy. I was eligible for a promotion in rank that year and did not get it. My annual fitness report included these words: "Though his cultural work is excellent, and he seems to know everyone worth knowing in the Spanish intellectual and artistic worlds, he has occasionally been uncooperative with other Embassy staff; he harbors certain radical religious leanings." Who would have thought that the Inquisition, long gone in Spain, was alive in the United States Embassy?

The story has a happy ending. This boss of mine left Spain shortly after our discussion when he got drunk and insulted a Spanish government official at, of all places, the embassy Christmas party he had wanted me to organize. To be respectful, I had attended and was nearby when I heard him trying to explain a theory of his that Americans and Spaniards have differing attitudes as to what constitutes truth. He might have had some subtle, philosophical point to make, but his Spanish was poor and he got more and more entangled and ended up saying more than he meant.

"Are you calling Spaniards 'liars'?" the irate Spanish official finally asked. The next morning there was a phone call from the Spanish foreign minister to the ambassador, and an hour later my boss was on his way out of the country on the first flight out of Madrid's Barajas Airport. A number of us stood outside the embassy as he was carted off in an official embassy car. I waved goodbye perhaps more enthusiastically than the rest.

Luckily for me, his replacement knew the whole story. Upon arrival, he immediately requested that I be promoted, and I was and, indeed, was promoted a year later again, so I was entirely vindicated and happy in my work again. And doubly glad that this had been accomplished without my compromising on an issue of importance to me.

And this was good because, despite my affection for Spain, the embassy had been a kind of sanctuary for me from some of its extremes. For example, no one in Spain then but Catholics could practice their faith openly. The fraternal order of Masons, perhaps even more than Jews and Protestants, was under constant observation. For Jews, an unidentified apartment in a nondescript building in downtown Madrid was the only place of worship. Nothing in the street and not even anything on the door of the apartment suggested that there was a synagogue within. The unholy concordat between the Franco government and Rome, under which Franco had the power to appoint bishops so long as the church had exclusive religious dominion over Spain, is something the church should have rejected—that is, if it was interested in being Christian rather than simply powerful.

Today's Spain can take credit for becoming a nation where state and church are increasingly becoming separate spheres. One sees this in the debate about removing crucifixes from public schools, long overdue. Spain still has a long way to go, but at least there is freedom of worship for all religions. Anti-Semitism still exists, but the country is a much more congenial place for Jews and other non-Catholics than it was during the four years I served with the embassy.

During my embassy days, I would find the processions of Semana Santa (Holy Week) positively terrifying because of their official nature, with soldiers goose-stepping like Nazis and pointy masked, robed figures looking exactly like the Ku Klux Klan— though much more fashionably arrayed in a brilliant purple. Today, because they are not so much functions of the state, I can look at these processions as interesting from a folkloric or anthropological perspective. Like anyone else, I enjoy a parade.

Jews feel more welcome in Spain today than at any time since the Inquisition and the expulsion, and they are increasingly to be found in the country participating in national life and discovering the threads of Jewish language and culture still to be found in the fabric of Spain.

An American scholar I met in Spain during my embassy days was focusing on the origins of the Friday, the 13th taboo in much of western culture—though friends tell me that, at least today, Tuesday, not Friday, the 13th is considered the unlucky day in Spain.

But elsewhere, surely in the United States, it is definitely Friday. There has been a regular franchise of awful *Friday the 13th* slasher movies that teenagers favor. In each of these movies horrible things happen on Friday, the 13th. There are buildings in the United States that do not have a 13th floor. There are commercial airliners that do not have a 13th row. When a Friday, the 13th occurs (at least once, but never more than three times a year) everyone is extra careful, there is much to do about it in the media, and when, as is inevitable, something awful happens to someone, this is presented as proof of that date's terrible powers. Ironically, because of precautions taken by many on any Friday, the thirteenth, the accident rate on such a day is always actually lower.

Some Christians believe that the fear of Friday, the 13th stems from Judas being the 13th in Jesus' band

and Jesus being crucified on a Friday. The American scholar working on this subject had a different view. He believed that the Friday the 13th taboo had its origins in the Spanish Inquisition. Friday at sundown is the beginning of the Jewish Sabbath, when Jews customarily light candles. The church and its spies would be watching the homes of supposed converts to see if lights could be detected through the thick curtains. As for thirteen, it was the Jewish theologian, philosopher, medical doctor, and poet, Moses Maimonides—whose early life was spent in Cordoba, Spain, where there is a bust of him in a lovely plaza— who first expounded the Thirteen Jewish Principles of Faith. Thirteen, in Judaism, is, therefore, not a bad number; quite the contrary. Boys and girls have their bar and bat mitzvahs at thirteen. Thirteen is the age at which a young Jew may first be called to read from the Torah, a rite of passage connoting the beginning of maturity. Young Jews look forward to being thirteen the way the young everywhere look forward to being old enough to drink and to drive.

It does not seem accidental that, during the Spanish Inquisition, when a Jew's conversion to Catholicism was considered suspect, he would be tortured until he confessed to "siguiendo en su trece" (continuing with his thirteen) and then likely burned at the stake. Thus, this American scholar's belief that the Friday the thirteenth taboo originated in the Spanish Inquisition may have been valid. In Spain, during the Inquisition, Fridays and thirteens could bring an individual much sorrow if not death.

This same scholar was looking into the influence of Hebrew on Spanish. He was particularly interested in the word "*desmazelado*," an antique term to be sure, common in Ladino though not in contemporary Spanish, but, he insisted, derived from the Hebrew word "*mazel.*" Jews commonly say "*Mazel tov*" at times of celebration, such as weddings, bar mitzvahs, or when one has achieved some success. "*Mazel*" means star. "*Tov*" means good. A literal translation of mazel tov would be "good star," but its everyday meaning is "congratulations." Thus, "*desmazelado*" would be essentially the opposite. A "*desmazelado*" would be one who has not had the benefit of a good or lucky star, who has, in effect, experienced bad luck. Those persecuted by the Inquisition were definitely *desmazelados*.

Another American scholar working in Spain during my years there was looking into Christopher Columbus' Jewish roots. I was surprised to learn that this was an issue of interest. Growing up in a largely Italian-American area of New York City, I had experienced Columbus Day as an Italian holiday. Little, if anything, was said about Spain. The Columbus Day parade was organized by Italian-Americans, and all the politicians were sure to march in it to curry favor, and votes, from Italian-Americans. I was surprised when I first arrived in Spain to hear Columbus Day referred to as "Dia de la Hispanidad" (Spanish Day) and, even more powerfully, "Dia de la Raza" (Day of the Race). Little, if anything, was said about Italy. It is a cliché but true that whoever has the power of numbers writes the history. Today we have so many Spaniards and Latin Americans living in the United States that there is already emerging a cultural war between them and the Italian-Americans over Columbus' identity and who will officiate over the Columbus Day parade.

The American scholar added a further, complicating note. "If there were more Jews," he said, "Columbus would be Jewish." This surprised me, but this gentleman went on to write a book arguing that Columbus' primary identity was Jewish. His family had fled the Spanish Inquisition and settled in Genoa, Italy. They were Marranos (an ugly word to say the least; while it refers to secret Jews, its literal meaning is "swine"). This scholar would argue in his book that it was not incidental that Columbus first sailed in 1492, the year of the expulsion. He believed that Columbus never planned to reach India but was, instead, seeking a land of refuge for his co-religionists in the New World. He told me that Columbus' navigator was openly Jewish and, further, that Columbus wrote to his son, under a kind of house arrest in Salamanca to guarantee the return of his father, partly in Hebrew.

I found this scholar's theories rather fanciful, but in recent years several new books have been published advancing similar arguments. One was written by Simon Wiesenthal, the famous Nazi hunter. I guess my own view is that Columbus should probably be regarded as all three: Spanish, Italian, and Jewish—the very embodiment of the multiculturalism and diversity so celebrated today in the United States.

But claiming Columbus, or a piece of him, can be a mixed blessing. First, Columbus didn't really discover anything. Assuming those of us in the West need to believe that a European discovered America, we already have archeological evidence that Norsemen landed in the New World five hundred years before Columbus. And there is increasing speculation that the Chinese may have landed on the Pacific Coast of what is now the United States long before the Norsemen or Columbus. Not to mention that clearly it was the indigenous people who discovered America—some fifty thousand years before the Chinese, the Norsemen, and Columbus, so they, if anyone, are the ones who deserve the credit. And what fools we are to imagine native peoples exclaiming with joy when they met Columbus: "Thank you so much for discovering us, Chris. We can't wait for you to destroy our religion and culture and give us your smallpox and syphilis, which will kill, they say, only ten million of us." Recently the city council of Berkeley, California voted to no longer call October 12th "Columbus Day." Henceforth it will be known as "Indigenous Peoples Day." Not a bad idea—though I do rather admire the statuary in the Plaza de Colón ("Colón" is Spanish for Columbus) in Madrid and in Columbus Circle in New York City.

And there is probably enough of the proud Jew in me—forgive this bit of chauvinist silliness—that delights in the notion that the man who "discovered America" had Jewish roots or may even have been secretly Jewish. We already can claim Einstein, Freud, and Marx, so why not Columbus too? A little bit, anyway. There may be injustice in Italians and Spaniards having for so many years taken near exclusive credit for Columbus and his alleged exploits, but we Jews needn't repeat their errors.

Whatever Columbus' antecedents, Spain has, in recent years, taken considerable pride in its Jewish heritage. One can commonly find recorded Ladino tunes in Spanish stores and a multitude of books on Jews and Spain. And much is made of archeological monuments such as the El Transito synagogue in Toledo, the mikvah (ritual bath) discovered in Gerona, and the various juderias (Jewish neighborhoods) in Spanish cities. But how much better it would have been for Jews, and for Spain as well, had the Inquisition and expulsion never taken place. It is always better to preserve cultures than to create museums celebrating them after they have been destroyed.

Nevertheless, Spain is a much more likeable, democratic, and cosmopolitan place today than during my years with the embassy in the 1960s. It is probable that were I to visit that bar in Asturias today, no one—even knowing I am Jewish—would look for my horns. At least, I would hope not. Then again, I might almost wish to have such horns; they could be extremely useful in a fight. Also, we Jews have always been stubbornly non-conformist, so having horns might be a way of continuing that tradition. Though I have never entertained any "Chosen People" ideas, it's always nice to be a little special.

# *Comida y propina*
## (Food and Tipping)

BEFORE ENTERING the diplomatic service I was a graduate student in American Studies at the University of Minnesota. Minneapolis was then, in many ways, still "Zenith," the name Sinclair Lewis, America's first Nobel in Literature, favored when writing about the city in such novels as *Main Street, Dodsworth,* and *Babbitt.* He meant "Zenith" ironically. It means "the top" or "the best." By exaggerating Minneapolis' appeal so markedly Lewis meant to signify everything parochial about it and the Midwestern United States. Lewis would surely have been interested in a certain restaurant in Minneapolis that claimed to be Italian. I went there one day seeking cosmopolitan relief from Minnesota's wholesome ordinariness. I ordered pasta, and the waiter brought me a plate of noodles. When I asked "Where's the sauce?" he said, "Oh, you want sauce too?" He handed me a bottle of ketchup. It was a scene straight out of Garrison Keillor's show *A Prairie Home Companion.*

Americans in those days ate not for pleasure but to stay alive. It wasn't just McDonald's and fast food; it was also that the wrong Brits had crossed the ocean to what became the United States, and we Americans were still in their thrall. We had had a political revolution but not a gastronomic one. Good food was too sensual an idea for Americans, almost sinful. If only New England's early settlers had been fun-loving instead of those dour Puritans.

The situation has largely changed today in the United States. In addition to a multitude of other cosmopolitan influences (the United States is, after all, the United Nations in miniature), we Americans have become more of a Hispanic culture, with vast immigration especially from Latin America. These immigrants have been instructing we gringo Yankees in how to enjoy ourselves. Also, New York, not Paris (where there are great museums but little contemporary artistic excitement) has been the center of the art world for decades now, and good food and wine have accompanied this cultural flowering. But there are splendid restaurants everywhere, and California wines get better every year. Indeed, ordinary American restaurants and wines are better than ordinary French restaurants and wines, though the best American restaurants and wines may not yet equal their French counterparts. But the best Spanish ones already surpass the best French ones—though I have noted a tendency in Spanish restaurants near the French border to compromise honest native food with fussy, French pretensions. Spaniards should resist this with all their power. French food and wines are, in general, the most overrated in the world.

This was demonstrated by the 2010 list of the best restaurants in the world, selected by an association of eight hundred and six chefs, restaurant critics, restaurant owners, and gourmands. On that list three of the five best restaurants were Spanish and another was in the top ten. And the list didn't include El Bulli, the restaurant on Spain's Costa Brava which for many years has reigned as the number one restaurant in the world, because El Bulli was soon to close its doors and become some kind of gastronomic museum. The top French restaurant on the list occupied the eleventh position. And, surprise: an American restaurant was found among the top ten on the list. Prejudices of all kinds in favor of French cuisine and against Spanish cuisine were overcome by Spain's striking prominence on the list. But having spent not only considerable time in Spain but in France as well, it didn't surprise me.

It was in Spain that I first discovered a world of gastronomic pleasure, and to this day I am an habitué of Spanish cuisine. At home in New Jersey my family and I cook regularly with olive oil and garlic, and some of our favorite dishes are *gambas al ajillo* (garlic shrimp), gazpacho, *chuletas de cordero* (lamb chops) with lots of garlic, and *alcochofas salteadas* (artichokes with bits of ham). It is our family custom to make a paella on New Year's Eve. Sweet melon with salty Iberian ham is one of the world's great edible inventions, and Spanish *chorizo* sausage is nowhere surpassed, nor is that marvelously dry and subtle manchego cheese, nor olives stuffed with anchovies. Spanish restaurants in the United States are pale imitations of their counterparts in Spain. Crossing the Atlantic seems to have diluted their flavor. My family makes better Spanish food at home than that generally available in Spanish restaurants in the United States.

Olive oil has entered the American diet in a major way in recent years, partly because of its supposed health benefits—the good fat, not the bad; doesn't clog your arteries. And now the latest: olive oil, it has been reported in a medical study, suppresses the onset of Alzheimer's disease. Something about it knits one's neurons together, greases one's brain, I suppose.

Which is fine, except that eating because something is delicious, instead of for its alleged health benefits, is, I think, more important to happiness and even health, whatever the cardiologists and neurologists say. Doctors and medical scientists change their minds every ten minutes anyway. Garlic has also been touted for lowering blood pressure and cholesterol, but most Americans still will not cook with it or tolerate it in restaurants, healthy or not. They fear that, eating garlic, because of the strongly scented breath it provokes, will alienate friends and drive away intimates. There is a restaurant in San Francisco called "The Stinking Rose" that specializes in dishes with garlic in them, as if such cooking is so unusual as to give name to a restaurant. There could not be a restaurant in Spain with such a name, garlic being a normal part of everyone's diet. The Stinking Rose name does offer fair warning to Americans: garlic may be pretty as a rose, but if you eat it your breath will stink.

"Stink" was the word that occurred to me when I arrived in Spain and was at my first embassy cocktail party. I was chatting with one of the ambassador's

The author seated at his desk in the American Embassy in Madrid.

Spanish guests. Or trying to. His breath was fierce. And Spaniards stand close to others when speaking. Between this gentleman's breath and his standing so close I felt dizzy. My eyes crossed trying to keep him in focus. I backed up slowly, not wishing to offend, but he followed, keeping the distance between us constant. No one ever stands so close in the United States unless they have amorous or bellicose intentions.

As soon as I could decently manage, I excused myself from this gentleman and, anticipating relief, approached a very pretty Spanish woman only to discover that her breath was equally insupportable and she stood just as close. Not to mention that, upon our being introduced, she kissed me on both cheeks. Not being used to this familiar form of Spanish greeting, I entertained certain fantasies, though these were dispelled as I realized that such affection and closeness is just how Spaniards are. But how could so glamorous a woman have such lethal breath?

I thought then that these Spaniards must practice uncommonly poor oral hygiene. Surely, they did not floss; surely they needed to invest in quantities of industrial strength mouthwash. Of course, since everyone eats garlic regularly in Spain, no one notices anything repugnant about the breath of others. Everyone has the same perfectly fine garlic scented breath.

But I only learned this when I myself became a garlic aficionado. Ever since, I have been unable to imagine good food without it. One does, of course, run the risk of finding one's American acquaintances restricted to fellow eaters of garlic. Luckily my wife and children like garlic flavored food as much as I do. I believe I could operate a profitable business in the United States manufacturing pins that say I EAT GARLIC. These would be worn like religious talismans, much like a Cross or Star of David. Bumper stickers for cars might also sell well. Advertising their gastronomic proclivities, garlic eaters would assure non-garlic eaters that their "foul breath" was not a matter of sanitation. Were this not sufficient, garlic eaters could form social networks, clubs, participate in e-mail chat rooms. Seeking mates, they might resort to the Personals in newspapers: *Elegant woman, late thirties, brunette, blue eyed, 5 foot 6, full figured, seeking long term relationship. Garlic eaters only. Box 234.*

Good coffee was something else I had never experienced before living in Spain. This was before the Starbucks Revolution in the United States and all the other coffee houses it spawned. As a student I never drank coffee except to stay awake while studying. It tasted like sulfuric acid and seemed entirely capable of burning a hole through one's stomach. Mark Twain used to refer to American coffee as "slumgullion." I don't know what it means precisely. I suppose the "slum" part offers a clue.

I began drinking coffee on arrival in Spain because it was so good, and there were all those dizzying choices: *café con leche* (coffee with milk), *cortado* (a small coffee with a whisper of milk that "cuts" the coffee), espresso, cappuccino (same as in America). And now this is widely true in the United States too. The coffee revolution happened, I believe, because traveling Americans experienced European coffee and, on their return to their country, would no longer tolerate American coffee. So now they and I drink coffee not as a drug to enable us to keep working but as a refreshing and delicious treat.

Today there are two kinds of coffee in the United States, good and bad. There is virtually a class distinction between those who seek lattes and those who drink slumgullion. The former costs considerably more. But it's not just an economic matter; it is political and cultural as well. It is hard to imagine George W. Bush sitting in a coffee house, but easy to imagine Barack Obama there. John Kerry may have lost the presidency in 2004 partly because he was perceived as a snob who probably drank "fancy" coffee instead of American rotgut. It went along with people thinking he was not 100% American because he spoke French. There is a long anti-intellectual tradition in the United States, and those who speak anything besides English and seek out good coffee are often thought of as effete intellectuals, egghead professors, that is, people like me. I never know whether, when pronouncing the name of something like the nation Chile properly—"cheelay" rather than "chilly" (cold) or "chili" (a food)—I will be thought by my fellow Americans to be putting on airs. If only English was, like Spanish, more phonetic.

The availability of good coffee in every Spanish bar suggests the world of difference between Spanish and American bars. A bar in Spain is usually a family-oriented place—sociable, safe, well-lit. All the generations go to the bar together. Grandma wants a coffee, Paco, a beer, Maria, a glass of wine, the children, ice creams or Fanta limones (a brand of soda) When I first arrived in Spain, I thought bars were social clubs. For a while I wondered where "the real bars" were.

Most American bars are dark, menacing places. Grandma would not feel safe, and the children would not be permitted to enter even when accompanied by their parents. There is no coffee or ice cream in American bars. Americans largely go to bars not to be in society but to drink and, often, to get drunk. One rarely sees drunks in Spain; one sees them too often in the streets of America.

When it comes to alcohol, Americans tend to be all or nothing. We are, after all, the country of Prohibition. We passed a constitutional amendment in the 1920s forbidding all alcoholic beverages and then had to undo it in the 1930s with another amendment. The 1930s amendment put the gangsters out of business.

Moralism with regard to alcohol may explain why bars are generally considered places of ill-repute in America. The woman seated alone in that bar must be "in business." Those fellows at that dark corner table must be mobsters. Fist fights break out in bars. Indeed, some men go to bars seeking a fist fight, as if a night out wouldn't be successful without receiving and delivering a quantity of lacerations and black eyes.

Some American men behave in bars as if the Old West is still alive. They delight in splintering chairs over other men's heads. They get drunk so as to express hostility and be violent. Large bars have bouncers to keep the peace. You don't behave, they *bounce* you out of there. I don't believe I've ever seen a bouncer in a Spanish bar.

The drinking age in the United States is currently twenty-one. So what do many young Americans do on their twenty-first birthday? They go out and get blind drunk. Instead of growing up with alcoholic beverages as something natural and normal, to be enjoyed rather than abused, they reach twenty-one and go crazy.

When I grew up the drinking age was eighteen, but I could not vote until I was twenty-one. Now

The author being interviewed on Radio España on his thoughts about Spanish cuisine.

these two rites of passage have been reversed. At eighteen you can help decide who will be president of the United States and you can serve in the military and get killed in a place like Iraq or Afghanistan, but you can't drink. Being Jewish I had the advantage of having some sweet wine on Friday nights almost from infancy as part of Sabbath observance. So I grew up thinking of alcoholic beverages as natural and pleasant, certainly not something that inspired in me bellicose attitudes. Today, I enjoy drinking wine, and, from time to time, I do get a bit inebriated. But, as I do, I become more, not less, sociable and pacific. At a party I may kiss every woman on the cheek and hug every man, but the last thing I would want to do is hit someone. That old 1960s adage, born in opposition to the Vietnam War, "Make love not war," would seem to apply to me especially when uninhibited. I rather wish it was universal in the United States. We would be a happier country. But Puritanism is still alive and well.

Here's an example of it. In American restaurants waiters come by regularly and ask customers, "Are you finished or are you still working on that?" *Working?!* Does one always have to be working, even while eating and spending a lot of money in a fine restaurant? You are enjoying a sensual delight, and they want to know whether you're still "working" on it? Would they ask you whether you were still working on it while smelling the flowers, listening to music, or making love? It is rather a utilitarian view of life. Do they think that if you are not working you are somehow sinful or, worse, wasting time? Nobody asks you if you are still "working on that" in a Spanish restaurant.

In Hollywood movie ratings, violence is more acceptable than sex or nudity. I think it may be, in part, because violence usually constitutes "hard work." You are "getting something done."

Every American, regardless of religious background, is a protestant (with a small "p"). What I mean is that we embody what the sociologist, Max Weber argued in his book, *The Protestant Ethic and the Spirit of Capitalism*, that under Calvinist Protestantism, the religion of the Puritans, one must not spend, just invest, because accumulated wealth is likely a sign that you are of the elect of God. Such an idea, which explains a figure like steel tycoon Andrew Carnegie, may have made us a rich and powerful country, but it doesn't make us happy. My own belief, helped along by my years in Spain, is that if there is a God she (yes "she!") wants us to be happy, and wealth is only incidental to happiness.

Another thing that would make the United States a happier country, I think, would be to rethink the whole issue of tipping. In Spain, tipping is something casual, just leaving the change from one's meal or bar tab on the table or counter. Waiters make most of their money through salary; if they make a little extra that's fine, but they're not especially dependent on tips for their livelihood. In the United States waiters are paid little or no salary. Their livelihoods are entirely dependent on tips. I once worked as a waiter and was paid a token one dollar per week—my real income was tips.

Tips can make the dining experience in the United States fraught with tension. Should one leave 15% of the total bill as a tip, 20%, or something in between? And should the percentage be based on the food and drink alone or the tax as well? In New Jersey, where I live, it is customary to leave 15%, but just across the Hudson River in New York City it's customary to leave 20%. One almost has to carry a pocket calculator to figure out how much to leave on the table as a tip in American restaurants. Some Americans do exactly that. And there is always stress about whether one has left enough of a tip or too much.

I hate the whole idea of tipping. It seems undemocratic, suggesting that the person receiving the tip belongs to a lower social class. He or she is not a professional but your temporary slave or, at least, a lower form of life. Also, there is the assumption that one will not get good service unless one "bribes" those serving you with a handsome tip.

I much prefer the system in most Asian countries where, without tipping, service is excellent. Indeed, tipping in Asia is considered an insult to professional integrity. I recall landing at Tokyo's Narita Airport, jumping in a taxi, and giving the driver ten percent over his bill when we arrived at my hotel. He returned the extra money to me, smiling but suggesting I had made a mistake. I tried to give him the tip several more times, with the same result: he firmly pushed the money back into my hand. The same thing happened when I attempted to tip the bell boy who carried my suitcase to my room. He looked at me strangely and walked out of my room without acknowledging the Yen I was holding out to him. At dinner, the same thing happened with my waiter. He ran after me into the street to place in my hands the tip money I had left on my table. It took those three experiences for me to learn that one does not, indeed *must* not, tip in Japan, and this certainly does not negatively affect service. It may even improve it. People in the service industries consider themselves professionals, not beggars.

I do wish the United States would follow the Asian model in terms of tipping. Add the fair amount—either in the direct cost of things or as a service charge—to any bill and then everyone can relax. Yes, tipping in Spain is more relaxed than tipping in the United States but I still see it as a vestige of feudalism; it makes unnecessary social distinctions between served and server that I abhor. I understand that during the Spanish Civil War, at least in Republican territory, there were bars and restaurants where even minimal tipping was not only discouraged but forbidden. Everyone, in every field of endeavor, was considered a worker and entitled to equal respect.

During my embassy days I had one experience with tipping I shall never forget. We had a fire in our Madrid house. Some Chinese-American friends were visiting and were cooking their specialty, Peking Duck. The duck, marinated for hours, was now suspended in the middle of the oven by a series of strings, the marinade sauce dripping below. Suddenly, the whole stove, inside and out, became a ball of flame. I hastily turned off and unhooked the butane tank, tossing it into the garden. If the flames had reached it, it might have exploded. Then I phoned the emergency number.

By the time the firemen arrived the oven fire had gone out, perhaps because there was no more gas feeding it and the duck, now a tiny black thing the size of a scorched sparrow, was cremated. I thanked the six firemen for coming but they continued to stand about in their Roman centurion fire hats. I had thought they would return immediately to the firehouse, but they just stood there. I figured the least I could do was offer some hospitality. I put out cheese and crackers and olives and chorizo. I put out soda and water, but when there was little interest in them I put out beer and wine and Scotch whiskey. I thought the firemen would say, "Thanks, no alcohol on duty," but they quickly drank everything I had just put out, so I put out more. My family and our somewhat chagrined Chinese American guests had joined us. A Spanish neighbor with whom I was friendly had also come over. We seemed to be having a party.

But didn't these firemen have other things to do? Maintenance work at the firehouse? Fires to put out? I was running out of supplies, but they still stood there. An hour went by. Finally, the chief signaled to the others and the firemen left. Each shook hands with me—rather gravely I thought. I had no idea at the time that they had left disappointed.

As my neighbor prepared to depart I asked him why the firemen had remained at our house so long when there was clearly no further danger. "What did you give them?" he asked.

"Well, you saw," I said: "food, drink, whatever I had."

"No," he said, "the tip."

"Tip?" I asked, incredulously. "In Spain one gives firemen—public officials—tips?"

"Not a lot," he said, "but something. They stayed because they were waiting for the tip. They were only eating and drinking to be sociable. Had you given them a little tip they would have left immediately and it would have saved you a fortune in food and drink." So, in this respect I prefer the American idea: don't tip public officials. If you did, it would be considered a form of corruption.

The next day my kindly neighbor left on my doorstep a beautifully wrapped little package. I untied the ribbon, and inside was a little plastic duck. From then on he would jokingly refer to me as "El Hombre del Pato" (Duck Man). I still have that duck. Indeed, it has been sitting on my desk in New Jersey as I wrote this story.

# Dr. Zhivago: Shooting a Movie in Spain

ONE MARCH MORNING in 1965 my embassy phone rang. "Mr. Rockland? This is John Palmer with Metro Goldwyn Mayer. We're making *Dr. Zhivago* here in Madrid. Perhaps you were aware of that."

I was not.

"Anyway," Palmer continued, "I wonder if you could help us: we're looking for an American boy—about four and a half. Do you know one?"

At first I thought Palmer was joking. Then I said, "Know one? I *have* one."

"*You* have a son who is about four and a half?"

"Four and a half next week."

"Splendid," Palmer said. "I wonder if I might send a car for him tomorrow. I'd like David to have a look at him."

I didn't know who David was but I arranged to take the day off from my embassy duties and phoned Jeffrey's nursery school to tell them he would not be there the next day.

At 9 in the morning a chauffeured black Humber pulled up on our street in Madrid and Jeffrey, his mother, and I piled into the back. The automobile headed out the Avenida de America. Half way to Barajas Airport a nondescript brick building hung over the freeway. I had passed under it many times, never knowing it was a film studio.

We were ushered into a large room, instantly discovering to our shock and dismay that there were some thirty couples with their little boys waiting, their chairs in a line along one wall. I had never seen any of these people before. Who would have thought there could be so many Americans in Madrid with four and a half year-old boys?

We had assumed MGM wanted Jeffrey himself for a single, quick shot, but in this room was a veritable army of competition. We thought of leaving but decided to wait a while and see what would happen.

So, we waited. And waited. My watch said 10:30. Then 11:00. If we and the other parents were restless, one can imagine how restless the little boys were. Jeffrey kept saying, "I'm bored. There's nothing to do here."

Prowling about the room, one of the boys discovered a large basket of chocolates on a table at the far end of the room. No one said the candy was for their consumption, but no one said it wasn't. Soon all the boys were gathered around the basket, quite peaceably dividing up the stash.

It was noon. Jeffrey's mother and I decided that if nothing happened by 12:30 we would leave.

At precisely 12:30, just as we were preparing to leave, the door opened and in came the great man himself. David was David Lean, the legendary film director, fresh from having made what is still my favorite film of all time, *Lawrence of Arabia,* partially shot in Spain (Seville is Damascus), and, before that, another great favorite of mine, *The Bridge on the River Kwai.* Lean was followed into the room by a group of staff members, including Freddie Young, his longtime, Oscar-winning cinematographer.

While the others leaned against the far wall, Lean paced up and down before the children and their parents, hands clasped behind his back like a British army officer. When he came to us he stopped and stared at Jeffrey before continuing on his way. On the way back along the line he stopped again in front of us. Jeffrey was a bit frightened being stared at this way. Who was this strange man and what did he want?

After canvassing the room one more time, Lean stopped yet again in front of us. He said to Jeffrey, "Say 'Daddy, are their wolves in the forest?'" Jeffrey looked like he was going to cry. "Just say it, son," Lean insisted. In his little voice Jeffrey, rather gamely I thought, said "Daddy, are their wolves in the forest?" Then he giggled.

Lean motioned Freddie Young over for a look. Young said one word: "Yes."

Lean said to me, "Please stay." Then he signaled to one of his assistants who clapped his hands and said in a clipped British accent, "You may all leave. Thank you very much indeed." The other families got up to leave, the parents disconsolately shuffling out, some looking back at us with what I took to be resentment. Who were we? What was so special about our son as compared with theirs?

We now learned that David Lean wanted Jeffrey for the role of Sasha, the son of Dr. Zhivago and his wife, Tonia. Jeffrey, with his big brown eyes and semi-Semitic features, looked like he could be the son of Omar Sharif, who is Egyptian, and Geraldine Chaplin, the half-Jewish daughter of Charlie Chaplin.

Lean escorted us into a little office where a striking-looking British film actor I had seen before in character roles was seated behind a desk. He had white hair and a great white beard. Lean assigned him to work with Jeffrey as a diction coach. He would be coming to our house in Madrid the next morning at 10. He advised us that John Palmer would also be coming by at noon with contracts to sign. "Remember," the diction coach said to Jeffrey before we parted: "'Daddy, are there wolves in the forest?'" putting the accent on wolves. He told us to work with Jeffrey on the line.

That evening, at home, we did exactly that. But after a few times, Jeffrey, not that long out of diapers, said, "That's cocky. I don't want to say it anymore." When we told him it was important he keep at it, he said, "What's 'wolves?'" We realized he was exhausted and might do better just to get a good night's sleep so as to be rested when his coach arrived. We didn't want to tell him what a wolf was for fear he would have a nightmare.

When Jeffrey's diction coach arrived the next day he wisely let Jeffrey do what he had craved from the first moment he'd met the man: touch his long white beard. We learned that Jeffrey would actually

Resting between shots during the filming of *Doctor Zhivago*. The "father," Omar Sharif, is on the right, the "mother," Geraldine Chaplin holds the author's son, Jeffrey. The "grandfather," Sir Ralph Richardson, is seated behind the others. In the background, facing the camera, is David Lean, the director of the film.

have twelve lines in the film, "Daddy, are there wolves in the forest?" being just one of them. The coach began working with Jeffrey on several of them. Though born in Minnesota and having lived in Washington, Buenos Aires, and Madrid, Jeffrey had picked up his parents' New York accents. The coach wanted him to have a more generic American accent. He told us that a British child had first been chosen for the Sasha part but his voice had been judged "overly precious. We want a strong voice, but New York's a bit *too* strong."

John Palmer arrived, as promised, at noon. He had two copies of a contract indicating that Jeffrey would be paid $26 a day. However little that seems today, it was then equal to my daily earnings as a diplomat, and Jeffrey was, after all, a little boy. It would be possible to put away a tidy sum towards his university education. Since either Jeffrey's mother or I would have to be with him every day he worked, we asked to be paid another $26. Palmer said, "Oh, it's not necessary you be there. We'll attend to the lad." Sure, I thought. I could just imagine Jeffrey playing around high power lines or being run over by a crane and no one— not even his movie father or mother— looking after him. Reluctantly, Palmer agreed to the other $26. Later we would learn that we probably could easily have gotten $100 for Jeffrey and another $100 for the parent accompanying him, but we were too smitten by the Hollywood mystique to ask.

John Palmer was Executive Producer of the film. Carlo Ponti, Sophia Loren's husband, would be listed in the credits as Producer but had nothing to do with the making of the movie. Apparently, when Nobel Prize winner Boris Pasternak's great novel was spirited out of Russia, it first appeared in the West in Italian. Ponti purchased the film rights and sold them to MGM for a hefty sum and the understanding that he would have the title of Producer.

John Palmer did all the actual work. He and his staff signed up the actors, paid the extras, rented or commissioned the sewing of Russian army uniforms, hired horses, hired attendants to feed them, rented studios, supervised the accountants, and dispensed money to an army of Spanish carpenters who were building Moscow on the plains outside Madrid.

This was a huge set, half a kilometer long. Most of the buildings lining the street were mere facades, but the Zhivago house at the end of the street had aspects of a real structure and was almost functional. Fully functional was the trolley line laid down the center of the set—real tracks, a real trolley, and overhead electric wires. Making a movie such as *Zhivago* can be almost as technical as putting a man on the moon. Indeed, when MGM was shooting at night the blinding lights and cranes made the set look like a space launch site.

Most viewers of the film can't believe it could have been made almost entirely in sunny, warm Spain because of the snow on the Moscow set and elsewhere. The snow drifts in the film are constructed of plaster, with quantities of white marble dust sprinkled elsewhere. However, for one scene, where Zhivago wades through waist high snow, Omar flew to Finland with a film crew.

In the years I was with the American Embassy, Spain was a mecca for big production movies. Out on the plains beyond Madrid faux cities were regularly built of canvas and wood—ancient Rome, the Egypt of the Pharaohs, Jerusalem in the time of King David. These were generally movies full of action: chariot races, bloody wars, sacking and pillaging, casts of thousands.

Spain was a poor country then. You could get huge sets built for a fraction of what they would have cost back in the United States. Carpenters were paid five dollars a day. Extras would also be paid five dollars a day. *Dr. Zhivago*, at $14 million dollars, was the most expensive film ever made up till 1965, but it would have cost many millions more if made in Hollywood or Britain.

In more recent times big picture makers have stopped coming to Spain because of the increased cost. This happened in concert with fine movies being made in Spain by Spaniards, and one wonders whether this was wholly coincidental. One increasingly hears the names of directors such as Saura and Almódivar, actors such as Javier Bardem and Penelope Cruz.

But in my embassy years it was mostly big spectacles being made in Spain by foreign directors, including several Charles Bronson movies. Except for *Zhivago*, which won five Academy Awards and was nominated for five more, none of these films were memorable. At the Embassy we were only subliminally aware of this filmmaking activity; there'd be pictures in the newspaper of Carthage or Troy being erected or torn down.

Or an American actor would get into trouble. I was once sent downtown to Madrid's Plaza Hotel to calm the actor, Broderick Crawford, who was drunk and tearing his room apart. I asked the people at the front desk to give me a few minutes with him to see if I could preclude their having to call the police. I had so admired Crawford's work as Willie Stark in *All The King's Men,* but here I was holding him up and making him down cup after cup of black coffee and telling him to cool it and pay for the damage he had caused.

The alternative, I told him, was jail. I wasn't just protecting Crawford; the embassy wanted as little bad press about Americans as possible.

Jeffrey's participation in *Dr. Zhivago* was divided between Madrid and Soria, a small provincial capitol in the north of Spain. The Madrid sequences were shot either in the studio, on the Moscow set, or in the Delicias train station, which was used for the footage where the Zhivago family escapes Moscow for their country property beyond the Ural Mountains. These shots could only be made in the middle of the night when the train station was not in use. Nightly set up and clean up took forever, though the huge posters of Lenin and Trotsky high on the walls of the train shed remained up during the days MGM was shooting there. I always wondered what the average Spaniard would think when he got off a train at Delicias Station and was greeted by the Russian Revolution—in Franco Spain, no less.

We demanded, and got, a trailer for Jeffrey outside the train station so he could get some rest between takes. Much of filmmaking is simply waiting while the director, head cameraman, lighting supervisor, and chief sound engineer confer. It can take seven hours to properly light a set for one shot. Filmmaking is not glamorous; it's akin to watching paint dry or grass grow. We would arrive at the trailer at about 8:00 p.m. each evening and put Jeffrey to bed until he was called, usually at about 3:00 a.m. The script called for Sasha to be asleep as Dr. Zhivago and his family board a cattle car. Jeffrey's "acting" was superb. In the shots that finally made it into the movie he actually *was* asleep in Omar Sharif's arms.

The long sequences inside the cattle car were actually shot in the studio on the Avenida de America. The inside of the cattle car was fabricated as a set and men, at opposite ends of the "car," rocked it with levers to simulate train travel, the sounds of train wheels on rails put in later. The main problem was keeping the actors cool in their winter clothes and furs during hot Madrid weather. You couldn't have sweat running down their faces during a Russian winter. There were huge cooling devices in the studio. In one shot Dr. Zhivago opens a little window in the car and urges Sasha to look out at the snow covered Urals. What Sasha sees was actually filmed from a moving train in the Canadian Rockies.

Jeffrey was supposed to be in a scene with Alec Guinness, who plays Zhivago's half-brother, the policeman, Yevgraf, and appeared regularly in David Lean movies, including *Lawrence of Arabia* and *Bridge on the River Kwai*. Jeffrey was to be in a crib in the Zhivago house, and Guinness was to lean over and ruffle his young nephew's hair. But Jeffrey had caught a wretched cold during the Delicias train station shooting, and we were afraid that if we let him work now, he might come down with pneumonia. The shot was postponed and finally cancelled when Guinness departed for work on another film. It was amusing that our little son had held up the great Alec Guinness.

The scenes beyond the Urals were shot outside Soria. An interesting set had been created—a house with two faces. One side was its summer face, the other its winter, with quantities of ice made out of clear plastic. Zhivago is with his family, including Jeffrey, on the summer side of the house and, later, with his lover, played by Julie Christie, on the winter side. A multitude of daffodil bulbs planted the previous fall so as to be in bloom for the summer side shooting rotted because the Spanish winter had been too mild. Plastic ones replaced them, except for one real daffodil that was used for a close-up. The color yellow is prominent in the movie, suggesting the golden haired Lara, played by Julie Christie.

One evening I sat around in the lobby of the hotel in Soria with Christie, Jeffrey asleep in our room upstairs. When I saw the movie *Darling,* for which Christie won the Oscar for best actress, I was absolutely smitten with her. It was now hard to believe that the rather ordinary young woman I was talking with in the lobby of that Soria hotel was actually the Julie Christie I had been in love with. Of course, when I next saw her on the screen, in *Dr. Zhivago,* I fell in love all over again. There are people with a natural charisma, "the shine" as the actress Meryl Streep once described it to me, that only comes out on the screen. Meryl starred in the movie, *One True Thing,* which was shot in my house in Morristown, New Jersey as the principal set. People think I have all sorts of Hollywood connections because of *Zhivago* and *One True Thing,* but the choice of our house for the latter was as much of a fluke as the choice of my son for the Sasha role in *Zhivago.*

Despite my enthusiasm for Julie Christie on the screen, I do wish I loved the movie itself more, especially since my son is in it. Men in general don't much care for *Zhivago*, and, like me, are often passionate about *Lawrence of Arabia*. Men find *Zhivago* a bit too sentimental. Women find it immensely romantic. For them it's the Russian *Gone With the Wind*, another movie women tend to love and men avoid. Beginning in the year 1983, eighteen years after *Zhivago* was released, I have had, as a university professor, a profusion of students with the name Lara or Larisa (Lara's nickname) in my classes. Their mothers must have been pregnant with them when they saw *Dr.* Zhivago and loved Julie Christie on the screen as much as I did, our affections enhanced by the gorgeous Lara musical theme that accompanied her presence, composed by Maurice Jarre, who wrote the music for and scored several David Lean movies.

Also in the lobby of that Soria hotel that evening were Tom Courtenay and David Lean. Courtenay plays the embittered revolutionary Strelnikov in the movie. Lean kept using a term I had never heard before: "WOGs." Finally, I asked him, "David, what's a WOG?"

"Well, "Lean said, "it's an acronym that stands for 'Wily Oriental Gentleman.' Some of you Americans might say 'Niggers.' We say WOGs."

"But who are the WOGS?" I insisted. "Black people aren't from the Orient."

"Oh," said Lean, "it's more or less a term for anyone who isn't white. The Africans, the Chinese, the Indians, the Egyptians."

"The Egyptians?!" I asked, incredulous, not stopping to point out that Egyptians and Indians are Caucasian, "but Omar is Egyptian. Doesn't that make Omar a WOG?"

"Well" said Lean, not breaking stride, "Omar isn't a real Egyptian." In retrospect, what Lean said about Sharif was not entirely unlike my telling Martin Luther King that he wasn't "a real Southerner."

Of course, Omar Sharif is indeed a real Egyptian, his naturally frizzy hair covered by a straight hair wig in *Dr. Zhivago*. I almost had the sense that for David Lean and for certain upper class Brits, anyone not British is a WOG and that Omar, who was appearing in his second Lean movie, was a kind of honorary Brit. It wouldn't have surprised me if David Lean had included Americans as WOGS, beginning with yours truly. One must remember that, during colonial days and in their immediate aftermath, the term "American," as used by the British, was a deprecatory term, a put down.

I felt protective of Omar. As a Jew and strong supporter of Israel I might have been wary of him but he was, after all, "my son's father" and a heckuva nice guy. Sir Ralph Richardson, Sasha's grandfather in the movie, was another story. Cold and distant, he seemed to ignore, if not actually resent, Jeffrey's presence. I don't think it had anything to do with Jeffrey. He just didn't seem to like children or perhaps it was that, as a professional actor, he didn't like sharing screen time with an amateur.

Omar was always affectionate with Jeffrey and often played with him off camera. My favorite scene with Jeffrey in it is when Zhivago comes home from World War I, running down the main street of the Moscow set to reunite with his family in the Zhivago family home. Sasha has never seen his father before and, afraid of this strange man, slaps him across the face when he leans over to kiss his son for the first time. That slap was filmed close to one hundred times. Each time, immediately after slapping Omar, Jeffrey would break into a smile. David Lean was exasperated. He would keep telling Jeffrey to look angry, and Jeffrey would look angry but only up to the slap itself. For him the whole thing was hilariously funny. He got to slap his movie father over and over. I doubt Omar enjoyed all those slaps very much. I'm sure Lean went crazy while editing the film deciding just where to cut the best of the shots and having twenty-four frames per second to choose among. If you were to watch the film carefully, you would note that, despite Lean's best efforts, there is still just the beginning of a smile on Jeffrey's lips just before the shot ends. To tell the truth, I never knew whether Jeffrey then fully understood that a movie was being made; everything on the set may have been just a game.

Recently, I sat down and watched all three and a half hours of *Zhivago* for the first time in many years. It brought back memories of Spain—of Madrid and Soria and of that curious group of people who had come together as a community to make a movie there. I had not seen any of them since *Zhivago* premiered to great fanfare in San Sebastian in very late 1965, and many of them have died since then. It was strange to see Jeffrey, this child of mine who already has four small children of his own and is considerably older than I was when the film was made, at age four and a half as Sasha Zhivago.

Two more things of possible interest: I discovered that the movie was about to come out with my son in the credits as "Geoffrey," the British spelling of Jeffrey. Glad I stopped that. Second, in the movie, eleven of Jeffrey's lines are in his voice. But the twelfth, the one he was taught first, "Daddy, are there wolves in the forest?" is in another voice, that of a little girl. Apparently, Jeffrey never could say the line properly and David Lean found a substitute to record that line back in a London studio and made it come out of Jeffrey's mouth. How strange it is to watch a movie and see one's young son say something and, in addition, it isn't even his voice. If I didn't mention this you probably wouldn't notice. Only a father could tell, even so long ago, that it isn't his son's voice.

# Lost in Translation

I WAS IN MY LATE TWENTIES and fairly innocent of Spain in particular and Latin culture in general when I first went to Spain, though I had earlier been posted to our embassy in Argentina. On arrival in Buenos Aires I heard everyone in the street referring to "Asia." I thought some catastrophe had struck that continent and asked people "What's happening in Asia?" They looked at me strangely. I bought all the newspapers at a kiosk on the Calle Florida, the city's lovely pedestrian only street, and went into a coffee shop to read them. I could find nothing of significance about Asia in the newspapers. Days passed before I realized that how Americans say "Asia" is exactly how Argentines pronounce "*ella*" (she). Spaniards say the word something like "eya." The double "l" is a "y" sound in Spain, in Argentine more like a "j".

Argentines today, after my years in Spain, routinely want to know if I learned my Spanish in Spain.

"Why do you ask?" I reply.

"Because," they say, "you speak with a Castilian accent." Of course, Spaniards think I have an Argentine accent. I tell citizens of both countries that my accent is actually pure New Jersey.

Differences in accent and pronunciation among Spanish speaking countries are paralleled by differences between the meanings of words. One of the first things I learned in Spain was that the verb "*coger*," never to be used in polite company in Argentina, is perfectly acceptable in Spain. In Argentina it means, plain and simple, "to fuck." In Spain it means to take hold of something. So, even within Spanish, there are important differences from country to country, and not just in accent or pronunciation. This should not have surprised me. In England, people are still learning to speak the proper English we in the "colonies" speak. Quite apart from their strange accents, to this day the Brits confuse "lorry" with "truck," "petrol" with "gasoline." Perhaps we Americans should send over cultural missionaries to straighten them out.

We must also contend with the fact that the same word may, in English and Spanish, mean very different things. I first became aware of this upon arrival in Madrid. Searching for a place where my family might live, I located a house in the Madrid neighborhood of Colonia de El Viso. An American family had previously lived there, the one that told me about the Romanian Nazis next door and left the ill-fated Pipo with me. Just before my prospective landlady and I signed the rental agreement, she told me that that family had been "*muy informal*" (translated literally : very informal).

"Glad to hear it," I told her.

She looked at me searchingly, her pen hesitating over the paper. Later I would learn that celebrating my predecessor's informality had nearly sabotaged the house rental. Americans can't imagine informality as anything but positive. What I thought of as easygoing and sincere she thought of as bad manners and incorrect, unreliable behavior.

Of course, the incident with my landlady occurred back when Spanish culture was in the grip of a very conservative church and the Franco dictatorship. Informality was not in the least prized. The Spain I knew in the 1960s was a stiff, buttoned up place. Men of any stature never went out of doors without wearing a jacket and tie, even on the hottest summer day. Neighbors on my little street never knew what to make of me when I came home from work at the embassy, took off my suit, and went outside in torn jeans and a dirty T-shirt to work on my car. For them, there were people who worked on cars and people who didn't; it was a matter of social class. What was I, an American diplomat, doing under my car, oil dripping down on my face?

Americans have always believed in a classless society. To put it another way, virtually everyone in our country considers themselves middle class, from the homeless person in the street to Bill Gates. We fought for our independence from Britain partly to rid ourselves of class distinctions. It is something of a myth that we succeeded, but we hold to it as an ideal.

Jeans, the national "uniform," is an expression of that ideal. With everyone wearing jeans it is largely impossible to discern social class. When I was a boy jeans were called "dungarees." The first part of that word, "dung," refers to manure. Dungarees were the trousers one put on to emulate cowboys,

The author seated at his desk at home in Madrid working on his doctoral dissertation on Domingo Faustino Sarmiento and the United States, eventually published by Princeton University Press. In front of him is a bust of Sarmiento.

one of whose regular tasks was shoveling manure. Thus "dungarees" implied people not too proud to work with their hands but still middle class. "Jeans" or, even more so, "designer jeans"—jeans with some celebrity's name stitched on one's rear—are virtually identical to dungarees but "classier." Or so those think who pay so much money for them. The most fashionable of these jeans come "stressed" from the store, appearing to the uninitiated as if they were plucked from a dumpster. And now the designer, Ralph Lauren—that clever devil—has come out with a new line of very expensive jeans called "dungarees." We've come full circle.

Today, everywhere in the world—with the exception of North Korea, where they are banned—jeans are worn. They are more of a symbol of American influence on universal culture than is McDonald's. However, in the Spain in which I lived, virtually no one wore them. And few were informal, utilizing either meaning of that word. It is testimony to how much democratic Spain has changed since my embassy years that everyone wears jeans and occasionally now I hear "informal" used positively. Regardless of the words utilized, it could be argued that today Spain is more informal than the United States.

I've noticed that Spaniards much more readily than when I was with the embassy use the familiar "*tu*" instead of "*usted*" when saying "you." Then it tended to be restricted to family and close friends. Also, Spaniards today often begin calling me "Michael" on our first meeting—or even before, in correspondence—and that is another sign of American-like informality. Whether a good idea or bad, this is one reason this American feels so much more comfortable in Spain than he did in the past. Let us hope, however, that as Spaniards increasingly use first names, this informality will not be exploited, as it is in America, by those trying to sell you something you do not want—such as another insurance policy.

One thing that took getting used to in Spanish as spoken in Spain (generally called "Castilian" now, to distinguish it from the various regional languages that were banned during the Franco dictatorship) is how so many Spanish words that appear to have

English equivalents seem much stronger, if not exaggerated, if said in English. We Americans must be careful in English to remember that these words do not have the same force or even meaning in Spanish, where they are everyday words. Literal translation is referred to in Spanish as *"traducciones de vaca"* (translations made by a cow). For example, there are the exclamations *"estupendo," "magnifico," "barbaro."* If one were to use these words in English, translating literally, they would be "stupendous," "magnificent," and "barbarous," words used only in the most extraordinary circumstances. Also, for us, something barbarous is an atrocity committed by barbarians, while for Spaniards, *"barbaro"* is usually a colloquial expression of delight or of approval. To the American eye and ear, much of Spanish, were it to be translated literally—always a mistake—would seem infected by inflation. These are examples of the "false friends" idea in translation—identical or similar words that appear in two languages but do not mean the same thing, sometimes even, quite the opposite.

My favorite in Spanish is *"constipado."* I thought it very curious during my early days in Spain that many people, especially in winter, would go about publicly announcing that they were *"constipado."* I was embarrassed for them and would look away. What a private, if not gross, thing to announce! What they meant was not that they were constipated but that they were suffering from colds, that they were, if you will, stuffed up at the other end of their bodies. There is a different word entirely in Spanish for constipated.

A conference on Spain and the United States organized by the author at El Escorial Monastery. On the right is Julian Marias, Spain's most distinguished philosopher at that time and a member of the Spanish Royal Academy. Marias also wrote several books on the United States which the author, in shirtsleeves in the picture, edited for publication in English.

Another word in Spanish that tickles me is *"embarazada."* It means pregnant, not embarrassed—though perhaps at one time it may have been a more delicate way to admit that one was pregnant if that was not desired.

I am reminded of the book by Guy Deutscher titled *Through the Language Glass: Why the World Looks Different in Other Languages.* At one point Deutscher writes that language "actually organizes habits of mind and influences perceptions in different cultures." I can testify to that. There are things I say every day in English that have no Spanish equivalents and vice versa. Thinking in another language is the only way to fully enter a culture.

To translate from another language one must fully understand the culture out of which its words have emerged or you will be translating literally, usually a mistake. I've always wondered what Hemingway had in mind in *For Whom The Bell Tolls* when his characters, especially Robert Jordan and Maria, speak in a kind of pigeon English, supposedly translated from the Spanish and laced with "thees" and "thous" Was Hemingway trying to communicate some of the flavor of Spanish in the English or just translating literally from the Spanish he would have placed in his characters' mouths. Frankly, I don't know. I remember reading the novel before I knew Spanish and finding the language charming. Now it seems rather corny.

In April of 2011 a lecturer at Princeton University of Spanish background, Antonio Calvo, killed himself after he had been suspended from the Spanish Department for reasons not entirely made public. But one reason he fell into disfavor seems to be his use of common expressions that are not in the least offensive in Spain but, when translated literally into English in the United States were taken to be insults and even threats. It would appear that misunderstandings from one language to another can, under certain circumstances, be dangerous, if not lethal. Humor, for example, is *sui generis*, limited by time and place. Today's joke can be tomorrow's insult. I have learned the hard way that what was funny to an earlier generation of students at my university is not funny today and, not always happily, I have tried to make adjustments.

Also, cultures, and the languages that embody them, are forever evolving and changing. For example, there is in progress in the United States a continual semantic redefinition of black people. When I was a child my parents would refer to "colored people." Coming of school age, I learned that "colored people" was a racist term and that the word "Negro" should be employed. With some discomfort, my parents agreed. But just having settled on "Negro," they and I were informed that this word was now racist and one should say "black"—with much discussion over whether the word should be capitalized or not; colors are normally not capitalized, ethnic groups are. Black people are obviously both though, of course, none of them are actually black. Brown, maybe, but not black.

There were two other ironies about "black." First, "black" was the term used during slavery days, so why was it now being championed? After slavery was abolished, "colored people" was actually considered a step up from "black." There was, and is, after all, the important National Association for the Advancement of Colored People (NAACP). Second, "Negro" means "black" in Spanish, so while we in the United States could switch to "black" from "Negro," being two different words, how could Spaniards be *au courant* in describing this group of Americans, since they had only one word, *"Negro,"* at their disposal. Having just settled down with "black," I was informed that the correct term was now "African-American." Which was fine with me, but I wasn't sure how to refer to a white friend of mine who had emigrated to the United States from South Africa. Was he not an "African-American?" Nor did I know how to refer to immigrants from African countries north of the Sahara, mostly Arabs, who are also Caucasians. Were they not also "African-Americans?" And what about black people who emigrate to the United States from the West Indies? To the chagrin occasionally of people who consider themselves African-Americans, they insist they are "Caribbean-Americans."

Recently, just after I had decided, despite arguments to the contrary, to adopt "African-American," sophisticates latched on to "People of Color" as the new term—which refers primarily to black people but also to anyone not classified as "white." There are several things wrong with this expression. First, with the possible exception of albinos, I have never seen a white person; we are all shades of beige or tan or brown. Second, every human being is colored something. And, third, "People of Color" sounds mighty like the very "Colored People" term I gave up as a child so as not to be thought of as racist. If we in the United States are confused about what terminology to use, one can only imagine how the issues I raise here—simply what to call a certain group of Americans—must puzzle Spaniards trying to discuss race in America, not to mention those translating from English to Spanish.

How should one racially designate President Barack Obama? His black father was from Kenya, his white mother grew up in Kansas. A Spanish friend asked me why we don't refer to him as "a mulatto," but Americans long ago gave up this word as a vestige of slavery and as particularly offensive because it was derived from the fact that mules are the product of the mating of donkeys and horses. It is interesting how in the presidential campaign of 2008 there were some Americans who considered Obama "too black," others who considered him "not black enough." This was primarily not a reference to color as to politics and culture. Often our problems and misunderstandings as human beings stem from simply not having the words to describe certain people or situations. Proper attention to semantics might very well preclude, or at least limit, human dissension and even warfare.

There is a movie I like whose entire plot hinges on a simple mistranslation: *The Ballad of Gregorio Cortez*, produced in 1982 and starring Edward James Olmos in the title role. Cortez is a Mexican-American accosted by the local sheriff, who is looking for a horse thief. Cortez is asked if he has a new "caballo" (which actually means "stallion," not horse). He responds "No, I have a new yegua" (a mare). The sheriff's deputy, with only a bit of Spanish and unaware of the male-female gender distinction between horses, tells the sheriff that Cortez refuses to cooperate in the investigation. Gunfire breaks out, and there will be many deaths before anyone comes to understand that, when it comes to an unfamiliar language, or one not fully mastered, a little knowledge can be a dangerous thing.

There is a book I confess to not having read, but I love its title: *El Delito de Traducir (The Crime of Translation)* by Julio-Cesar Santoyo. Translation *is* something of a "crime," come to think of it—albeit a necessary one. I've translated one book from Spanish into English without once feeling guilty that every word in that translation is mine—as if I had such callous disregard for its author as to feel free to "plagiarize" his work without apology. Let's face it: reading a book in translation is not reading the same book as the original. For example, reading a novel in English that was originally written in Spanish or some other language is to read a novel written by a translator based on the ideas of the original writer.

And this is, under the best of circumstances, a translation by someone both extremely knowledgeable, careful, and talented—an artist, since translation is primarily an art not a science. Of course, the "artist" part can be pushed too far: translators make up things—sometimes whole sentences, even paragraphs—that weren't in the original version. I have had writing of mine appear in various languages and, since the only language I know well is Spanish, it's only the Spanish editions of my work where I am able to read the translation before it appears in print, and I sometimes discover anomalies if not downright falsehoods and am able to point them out to the translator. I can't, for the most part, do this in other languages. Once something of mine appeared in Japanese. I'll never know to what extent the Japanese translator created a text entirely akin to what I had written or had used her imagination excessively.

Even names have different significance in different cultures. A certain name took a great deal of getting used to when I first arrived in Spain. Though I am not a Christian, I initially thought Spaniards who named their son "Jesus" must be guilty of blasphemy. Until recently in the United States, most Catholics have been of Irish or Italian or Polish origin, and few, if any, American Catholics would ever name their son "Jesus." They reserved this name for a being they considered divine. How could an ordinary boy be named Jesus? There was, for them, only one Jesus. Americans are beginning to get used to the name in common usage because of vast migrations from Latin America, which include a fair number of males named Jesus, but the name still seems strange to many of us.

I've asked Spanish friends with the name Jesus whether they feel any particular obligation to be well behaved. They laugh and say, "It's just a name," or "I'm a sinner like everyone else," or they joke: "Ironically, with this name I can get away with more." Still, the name Jesus, and its pronunciation in Spain, which sounds like "Hey Zeus" to the American ear (in English we say something that sounds like "Jeezus") takes some getting used to.

A personal note in this regard. My youngest child's name is Joshua. When he was born, Catholic friends would say, "You've given your son a very

Jewish name." That we had, though a very Christian name as well. Jesus and Joshua are the same name in different languages. Indeed Jesus' name was not Jesus, it was Yeheshuah. Jesus is Greek for Yeheshuah which is Hebrew for Joshua. I've always wondered why my Christian friends do not call Jesus by his own name instead of its Greek translation. It's a little like a certain Jose emigrating from Spain to the United States and deciding to call himself "Joseph" or "Joe" instead of sticking to Jose or if I were to move to Spain and insist my name was not Michael but "Miguel." Though if I may be so bold as to suggest, not calling Jesus by his proper name would seem to have, or should have, vastly greater significance to Christians.

Also sounding strange to Americans is when they meet Spanish men whose names are Jesus Maria or Jose Maria. How can a man carry the middle name "Maria," a woman's name? John Steinbeck had fun with this in his novel, *Sweet Thursday* (1954), one of whose key characters, of Hispanic background, a certain Jose Maria, he calls "Joseph and Mary." The same problem for Americans applies to Spanish women with the name Maria Jose or Maria Jesus. How can a woman have a man's middle name such as Jose or Jesus? We do have plenty of women named Mary Jo in the United States. Perhaps that was originally a shortening of Maria Jose. Mary Ann (Mary's mother supposedly having had the name Ann) might be another common example, though Ann is, of course, another feminine name, not a feminine name followed by a masculine one.

Americans do not associate anything religious with such names any more than do Spaniards.

Forgive my vulgarity, but there is a word in constant use in Spain today that I wish to discuss, "*coño*." I don't recall its universal use during my embassy days, but today it is everywhere and in every social context. If literally translated and utilized by a man in the United States it would cause his estrangement, if not permanent exile, from every woman in his life. It is probably our most taboo word in English: "cunt." Try using that word in the United States, whether in a small town in Iowa or in New York City, and you may not live to see another day. If one were to refer to a woman as a "cunt" this would be like calling her a whore multiplied one hundred times but also with specific derogatory reference to her genitals or the suggestion that she is nothing but her genitals. But, in Spain, "*coño*" is casually used even in polite society and with a hundred different meanings and, at the same time, none at all. People greet their best friends using this word or use it regularly at the beginning of sentences. It also seems to be a common exclamation, of little significance, such as "Oh, my!"

I have tried to explain this usage to key American women in my life—said that "*coño*" in Spain is generally not in the least offensive. But these efforts to demonstrate cultural relativism have failed miserably. Even mentioning that Spanish women friends— most of them professors and writers and quite as feminist in their orientation as anyone in the United States—do not seem at all offended by the constant use of "*coño*," has had no effect. I've asked Spanish women why they are not offended by this casual reference to female genitals, and they have laughed at me. "*Coño* may once have meant that," they tell me, "but it doesn't any more. It doesn't mean anything and certainly not anything offensive to women."

Ah, yes, language evolves. So much so that a Spanish scholar, Juan Manuel de la Prada, has written a respected book, in multiple printings, titled—you guessed it!—*Coños* (1995), with graphic illustrations throughout created by a distinguished female artist. The book is, broadly speaking, about Spanish culture.

Even my saying that the use of "*coño*" in Spain usually has no more negativity to it than, say, Argentines beginning their sentences with "*Que se yo*" (What do I know?) or Americans beginning their's with "Like" or "You know" or "Man" has not helped me with the American women in my life. Nor has it helped to point out that "*coño*" has no more significance than that plague infecting the speech of young American women these days, who cannot seem to say anything not preceded by "Oh my God" or in their e-mails and text messages, "omigod" or simply "O. M. G." That I know of, this expression is never a sign of religious devotion. It could, in fact, be regarded as a violation of the Third Commandment, to "not take the name of the Lord thy God in vain," but no one in the United States gives this a moment's thought. We have yet to hear preachers of various faiths inveighing against this usage from their pulpits. If they do, it will, no doubt, leave a host of young women temporarily mute.

Spaniards seem to forever be saying *"coño"* this and *"coño"* that, women employing it almost as much as men. During a recent trip to Spain I was actually greeted by an old friend who went much further. *"Coño,"* he said, advancing to embrace me, *"me cago en tu puta madre"* (which, if translated literally, means, "Cunt, I shit on your mother the whore."). My mother no longer being alive, my feelings were a little less violent than they might have been. And I tried to remember that the great Spanish film director, Buñuel, always insisted that Spanish was the most obscene language of all. Still, it wasn't until well after my friend explained that this was the ultimate greeting of endearment between friends that I was able to give up my strong desire, if not obligation, to strangle him on the spot.

I also realized that, in English, we sometimes use similarly vulgar terms in greeting friends. We may say, "How are you, you old son-of-a-bitch?" Or, much stronger, "How're doing, motherfucker?" Obviously one might use such terms in great anger, but, like *"Coño me cago en tu puta madre,"* they are usually expressions of affection. In a friendly context they don't mean that your friend's mother is a dog or that you are accusing him of having sex with her, but that you feel comfortable enough with him to use vulgar and even highly insulting words as testimony to your deep feelings for him and the mutual trust of friends.

Years ago, my wife and I were invited to dinner by Spanish friends at their home. The word *"coño"* flew about the room at regular intervals, despite the fact that the couple were serious Catholics and had both once served in the church. When our hosts were in the kitchen preparing to bring food out into the dining room, my wife turned to me and asked, "Are they saying what I think they're saying?"

I tried to explain that "*coño*" as used in Spain means something other than "cunt" if it means anything at all, that this is a common expression or interjection or exclamation, occasionally even a term of endearment, that its public expression virtually never has, in the Spanish mind, anything to do with women's genitals, that "*coño*," though I can think of no other way to translate it into English, simply does not mean "cunt" in Spain. She was, nevertheless, furious.

I could not begin to convince her that translating "*coño*" literally is incorrect, if not dangerous. It was all I could do to keep her from dashing out the door of their home. It remains a bone of contention between us to this day. She loves Spain as I do but finds the constant use of "*coño*" insupportable.

In Oslo, Norway a few years ago I went to see the wonderful 2003 Spanish movie *Mar Adentro* with Norwegian friends. In this film Ramon Sampedro, played by Javier Bardem, has been paralyzed from the neck down for almost thirty years and desires to simply end his life. Friends wish to help him, but he wants legal sanction so they will not be accused of a crime. The movie is based on an actual case that long wended its way through the Spanish courts.

At one point in the movie a priest who is similarly paraplegic, visits. He wishes to convince Sampedro that he has much to live for. The bedridden Sampedro is upstairs. The priest remains downstairs because it is impossible to transport his wheelchair above. In their shouted exchange, the priest, like any other Spaniard, utilizes "*coño*" as part of normal, colloquial Spanish. "Lord," I thought, "priests too!"

After the movie I asked my Norwegian friends if they were offended by anything in the priest's speech. While I had seen the film in Spanish, they had read the Norwegian subtitles. They knew of nothing offensive in what the priest said. "What did he say?" they demanded to know. I tried to explain as delicately as I could. They looked at me strangely as I, somewhat embarrassedly, told them about "*coño*" and "cunt." They assured me that there was nothing like that in the priest's speech as translated into Norwegian. At first I thought this might have been the work of Norwegian censors, but I soon concluded that those who crafted the subtitles wisely realized that the manner in which "*coño*" is generally used in Spain should not translate as anything sexual or offensive in Norwegian or any other language. I have since seen the movie with English subtitles and can report that the same thing is true of them as of the Norwegian ones, another example that translation and culture are intimately linked.

Finally, there is a Cuban restaurant in the town of Hoboken, New Jersey called La Isla (The Island) where I occasionally go with a daughter of mine who lives in that city. All the employees in the restaurant, men and women alike, wear T-shirts that simply say "*ño*" on them. I asked our waiter what this means. He told me that "*ño*," as I had begun to suspect, is short for "*coño*" in Cuba and that its usage is a source of national identity and even pride. I have attempted to share this further information—the Javier Bardem movie and the T-shirts in La Isla—with my wife but she refuses to hear anything about it. The same is true of many, though not all, American women friends and colleagues with whom I have discussed the issue. I write about it here as an example of cultural contrasts. Spaniards will understand what I am talking about. In my own country I hereby abandon the cause as, at least for the present, hopeless.

A related matter: in American English we have a host of words in common usage that were "dirty" in origin, or at least unmentionable in polite society, but have become parts of everyday speech just as in Spain. For example, when my students in the United States do not like something or someone they say "That sucks" or "he sucks" or "she sucks." When I explain to them that this term originated in expressions disparaging those who perform oral sex, they think I'm crazy. The connection that was once there has been lost.

The word "jock" is another case in point. At first, jock was short for jockstrap, the device protecting men's privates while playing sports. As a young athlete I never used that word in mixed company, nor did anyone else I knew. Later, "jock" came to mean any male athlete. But now it is used quite as frequently for female athletes, who never wear jockstraps. Today's young people obviously no longer associate the word "jock" with "jockstrap."

I should also report that such expressions as "Fuck you" "Oh, fuck!" and "fucking" as all purpose verbs, adjectives, adverbs, or exclamations have become almost universal in the United States, used, like coño, for virtually everything *but* sex, and, in becoming so widely used, have largely lost their power to offend. However, Americans *were* more than a bit surprised when former Vice President Dick Cheney told Senator Patrick Leahy of Vermont, right on the floor of the United States Senate, to "Go fuck yourself!"

I do think Americans curse utilizing religious terms more than Spaniards do. "God damn it!" or "Go to hell!" or "Jesus Christ!" are common expressions unconscious of religious significance or blasphemy except among fundamentalists and strict Catholics, whereas I have the sense they are taken more seriously in Spain. I do not hear them used often there. Each culture has its distinct taboos, and that's fine. We just have to be careful not to assume they are applicable elsewhere.

Worth mentioning are the differing challenges in learning Spanish and English. Except for the silent "h," the fact that all nouns in Spanish have gender (*la casa*, *el libro*), and the fact that the Spanish language "sadistically" offers two different verbs for the all important "to be" (*ser* and estar), English is harder to learn because it isn't, like Spanish, phonetic. For example, hearing the Spanish word "*bastante*" for the first time, one would know how to spell it. But pity the poor English learner when faced with the equivalent word, "enough." We pronounce it "enuff" but spell it in a way that looks nothing like it sounds. Not to mention that a considerable number of words in English sound alike, and in some cases are spelled identically, yet have different meanings. For example, "bear" (as in to carry), "bear" (the animal), "bare" (to be naked) and even the way southerners pronounce "beer" (the drink). If Hispanics learning English refused to learn the language until some phonetic rationality had been injected into it, I would sign their petition.

There is a related subject I want to discuss now, not language per se but body language. There is much that is lost in translation between Spain and the United States in how we comport ourselves in public.

Spain initiated me into being physically closer with people. In those days, American men never embraced. It was considered, well, unmanly. But living in Spain I was soon a great aficionado of the *abrazo*. It seemed a lovely thing for men to be physically intimate with male friends and relatives just as women were with other women—without this suggesting anything regarding sexual orientation.

I did get into difficulties with the *abrazo* when I first returned to the United States after my years at the Madrid embassy. My father and brother picked me up at Kennedy Airport in New York. As I advanced towards them, arms open, they backed up, alarmed. They must have been wondering what had happened to me in Spain that I intended to embrace them rather than to shake hands. Of course, these days in the United States, partly because of Latino influences, many men embrace. As mentioned elsewhere in this book, President Barack Obama is a great embracer or hugger, which has served to further popularize the *abrazo*.

Spain also taught me to kiss in a way I never had before. Some American men will socially kiss women, but it is always on one cheek. I can recall the first time I was introduced to a woman in Spain and proceeded to kiss her on one cheek. Our noses smacked into each other as I retreated and she moved toward the kiss on the other cheek. The blow brought tears to both our eyes. "*Que bruto!*" (what a brute you are) she exclaimed. I do hope that woman has forgiven me by now.

I think that before my Spanish experience I always kissed my daughters on the cheek but never my sons after they were more than a few years old. Spain changed that. Ever since, I routinely embrace and kiss all five of my now grown male and female children on the cheek, sometimes on both cheeks. In doing so, I fly in the face of traditional American custom. I remember when, as a boy, an Italian-American friend of mine complained of the embarrassment his father caused by publicly kissing him hello and goodbye. As my friend put it, "I wish he would cut it out. I'm an American." This fellow used to complain too about the dripping meatball sandwiches his mother sent along with him as his school lunch instead of the peanut butter and jelly sandwiches we "true Americans" always ate. Actually, I rather envied him his dripping meatball sandwiches. They surely tasted much better than my peanut butter and jelly sandwiches. They also seemed to complement the kisses bestowed on him by his father.

I guess that after so many years of experience of Spain I am a bit less "American" than I once was, certainly in terms of publicly expressing affection. However, I recall an incident when I was seeing my son Jeffrey off at New Jersey's Newark Airport. The same son who was in *Dr. Zhivago* as a child, he was then a professional ballet dancer, magnificently handsome and with a perfect body (if a father may brag). At first I had been disappointed in his dancing career, wondered whether it was sufficiently manly. Soon enough, however, I became a dance aficionado and found myself proud of his strength and grace. Ballet dancers aren't just performing artists; they are the world's greatest athletes.

Before Jeffrey went down the tunnel to his plane (this was before 9/11; travelers could be accompanied by non-travelers to their gates) we embraced and kissed each other on both cheeks. I stood there for a moment and then looked around me. People seemed to be gazing at me. Or I *thought* they were. Perhaps they weren't and it was just that elements of internalized homophobia I would have denied harboring had briefly reappeared in my thoughts. I imagined these people saw me as this middle aged guy saying goodbye to his young lover. Comic though the thought was—this was my son after all!—I was ashamed. Certainly, a father ought to feel comfortable about kissing goodbye a son of any age in any place in any country.

I recovered from my chagrin and, today, I'm a great hugger and a great kisser—females, males, children, old ladies, dogs, readers of my books—and my life is considerably the richer for it. I like doing these things so much I may already surpass my Spanish friends. If so, Spain's attractive, infectious culture is to blame.

# Kennedys

WHEN ANGIER BIDDLE DUKE arrived in Madrid as ambassador in 1965 the Kennedys began to arrive too. Duke had been close to the Kennedys. Prior to his assignment to Madrid he had served as chief of protocol in the State Department, the official handling visits of heads of state to Washington. It didn't hurt his ambitions that he was a major contributor to the Democratic Party. In the early 19th century, the Biddles were America's great banking family. Similarly, the Dukes made a fortune in tobacco, the name of the distinguished Duke University in North Carolina honoring their largesse. Angier was that rare thing: both a Biddle and a Duke.

With Duke, the embassy became a lively place, with interesting people arriving regularly from Washington and from Hollywood. I felt privileged, as a young diplomat, to be surrounded by so much glamour. It was one of the attractions of the diplomatic service. It would take time before I outgrew the illusion that being with famous or important people makes oneself famous or important too.

Duke, although incredibly rich, was plain spoken and unpretentious with a fine sense of humor. I recall being at a banquet with him in Madrid, up on the dais, and being anxious as to how to eat the chicken. I grew up lower middle class in the Bronx. In my family we had no reservations about picking up a piece of chicken with our hands. I even liked chewing on the bones and sucking out the marrow. My mother always said it was "the best part." But now I was in the diplomatic service; I couldn't do that, certainly not with Ambassador Duke sitting next to me.

I was startled when he picked up a piece of chicken with his hands and gnawed away at it. That was when I learned that the very rich and well born do not worry any more than do the poor about how they eat. Lower class people may eat casually because they don't know any better; upper class people because they couldn't care less what others think of them. It is only the bourgeois middle class that worries about their position in society and are anxious not to betray any lack of refinement. Determined to be "classy"—upper class not middle, at least in spirit if not financially—I too picked up a piece of chicken and gnawed at it.

"Good isn't it?" Duke said, smiling.

"It sure is, Mr. Ambassador," I said.

Edward Kennedy cared even less than Duke how he ate. Kennedy visited Madrid as a guest of Ambassador Duke in May, 1967, and I was asked to arrange a short talk and a Q and A for him at the University of Madrid, where I would do the interpreting. I was thrilled to spend time with one of the Kennedys, the closest thing we had in the United States in those days to royalty. The American people, despite their democratic principles—or perhaps because of them—have always had a secret desire for the very aristocracy we rejected in our revolution against the British. After the war, George Washington had to resist those who wished to crown him king.

Personally, I've never cared a bit about British royalty, but I did care very much about the Kennedys. I approached my meeting with Edward Kennedy with a certain awe. But when the ambassador introduced me to the senator in his office, Kennedy said, "Call me Teddy," immediately setting me at ease. Like Martin Luther King, Ted Kennedy was an example of American informality.

On the way to the university, in a chauffeured embassy car, Kennedy and I stopped off at a favorite restaurant of mine that no longer exists and had a long, Spanish mid-day meal with lots of wine. Not just the two of us: as an extension of his democratic ways, Kennedy had insisted that the chauffeur join us.

Kennedy's table manners were as "casual" as he was. Not only did he eat as he liked, without regard to certain proprieties, he even made off with a bit of food from my plate that I hadn't eaten. "You mind?" he asked, spearing a chunk of my lamb chop and then a small potato.

"Not a bit," I said.

He even sampled some of my flan after eating his own dessert, a large piece of chocolate cake. His eating habits probably account for why he grew so stout in later years. But, of course, he had always been the chubby Kennedy.

When it came time to leave the restaurant, at around 5 in the afternoon (our appointment at the university was for 5:30) guess who paid the bill? Like many rich people, the Kennedys had the habit of not carrying money with them. Perhaps that is how the rich get rich or, at least, stay rich. There are always people around them to take care of such "details." I was the one who took care of the details that day. I had to pay for the chauffeur's meal too, though he didn't realize I had and thanked Kennedy profusely for inviting him. That galled me.

But it was okay. It was an honor to take a Kennedy and a United States senator to lunch, though, in all modesty, I was, at that time, probably more qualified than he was to be a United States senator, which isn't saying much about the quality of senators. So I guess I envied him a bit. He seemed the perfect embodiment of the notion that life isn't fair. Over the decades, however, he would prove to be a very fine and well respected senator, one I could hardly connect in my mind with the young, rather uncouth guy I spent some time with many years before. He was a contradiction. As the cultural commentator, the late Dominick Dunne, would write about him, "He lived recklessly and often failed miserably in life, but he would also, if not at first, perform brilliantly in Congress."

Kennedy flattered me by asking that I consider joining his staff if ever I left the diplomatic service. I was keen. There was already discussion in the media in those days about Teddy someday being a candidate for president—so obsessed were Americans with finding another Kennedy to replace the murdered John—and I relished the thought of working in the White House. When his older brother, Robert was assassinated during the presidential campaign of 1968, Teddy was regarded as his natural replacement, if not immediately then soon. However, the Chappaquiddick incident a year later, on July 18, 1969, in which Kennedy was responsible for the drowning death of a young woman in his automobile, and of leaving the scene and not reporting the accident for eleven hours, would foreclose his chances and, by that time, I had opted out of political life anyway. You can't be both an artist and a politician, and my whole life might be seen as slowly sloughing off the latter in favor of the former.

Five years before Chappaquiddick, Kennedy was in a small plane crash en route to a campaign appearance in Massachusetts. It was a foggy night and the flight should never have been made. During the day in Madrid he was still wearing a cervical collar because, in the June, 1964 accident, he had broken his back though, luckily, without paralysis. He spent months in traction and would suffer from back pain the rest of his life. The Kennedy family certainly has had a penchant for tragedy. I think it was because they did not think that rules and limitations applied to them—which made them rather dashing and charming but dangerous to themselves and others.

Despite his back pain, Teddy was in great spirits that day in Madrid, though I suspect the wine had something to do with it. We got on very well. At lunch he wanted me to teach him some Spanish. I was reminded that he had been expelled from Harvard University for cheating on a Spanish examination. He had hired another student, whose Spanish was excellent, to take the examination for him. We continued with the Spanish lesson when we got back into the car, the chauffeur occasionally covering his mouth to hide his mirth at Kennedy's clumsy efforts. When we arrived at the university Kennedy vainly took off the cervical collar and left it in the car. "I don't want them seeing me with this," he said. Then he combed his hair carefully and seemed to immediately sober up—which is more than I could say for myself. He seemed to have a genius for appearing respectable when required, for transitioning from a drunken lunch to a public appearance.

At the university, after a few remarks by Kennedy about "how glad I am to be here" and "my love for Spain," the students began asking a series of questions. A key one was, "Senator Kennedy, what are your plans for the presidency?" Kennedy answered it in a timeworn political manner: "I am concentrating all my efforts on being a good senator from the State of Massachusetts." Politicians are always wary of peaking too early and usually run for office only when they can claim to have been urged to do so by "the people."

The highlight of the session concerned the war in Viet Nam. A young student stood up and said, "Tell us about *Tio Ben*."

I translated for Kennedy and he said, "What's he talking about? I haven't a clue."

I asked the young man what he meant. "We know why the United States is in Viet Nam," he said heatedly, "to get the rice." Now I understood: the reference was to that important brand of American rice, *Uncle Ben's*. "*Tio*" means uncle. The student saw the Viet Nam War as plain old colonialism, instead of what it was: a mistaken extension of Cold War thinking. He believed we needed rice and had gone to Viet Nam to take it away from the Vietnamese.

When I translated what the student had said, Kennedy laughed. "Tell him I don't know *what* we're doing in Viet Nam, but it isn't to get rice. The United States actually exports rice." Later, I checked on this and found that Kennedy was correct. Enough rice is grown in the State of Louisiana alone to take care of all American needs and then some.

Leaving the university at around 7 in the evening, Kennedy said, "That was fun, Michael. Let's get something to drink." That was the last thing I wanted to do, especially since my meager finances were likely to be taxed even more, but, of course, I went along with it. We found a bar and sat at the counter. Again, Kennedy's appetite—this time for tapas—was enormous. I think he tried one of everything. I was still full from our giant lunch, but I did quaff a good deal of wine with him. Luckily, for my family budget, the chauffeur had remained in the car, since Kennedy had said we would only be a few minutes. We were actually there over an hour, Kennedy becoming more voluble and enthusiastic with each passing moment. "Do you believe that 'Uncle Ben's' thing?" he kept asking, roaring with laughter. Kennedy would soon become an outspoken opponent of the Viet Nam War or, as the Vietnamese prefer to call it, "The American War."

Both of us somewhat drunk, we sang songs in the back of the limousine on the way back to the embassy. I don't remember just which songs but "Twenty-nine Bottles of Beer on the Wall" and "Row, Row, Row Your Boat" come to mind, he, I'm sure, just as proud of his terrible harmonizing as I was of mine. I managed to deliver him to Ambassador Duke's residence at the back of the embassy in one piece. Said Duke to Kennedy, "Great, just in time for cocktails." My heart sank. Any more to drink and I was going to pass out. Luckily, Duke took Kennedy by the arm, they disappeared into the residence, and I escaped and went home to recover.

I never saw Teddy Kennedy again, though I have often thought of what might have been had he become president of the United States—both for the country and for me. "The Road Not Taken" as Robert Frost put it in a famous poem. Kennedy died of brain cancer in August of 2009, the youngest of the great generation of Kennedy siblings and the last to die.

Over the years I found it difficult to connect the young Teddy Kennedy I had known in Madrid with the distinguished, aging and then sick senator. By the time he died he had served more time in the United States Senate than any living senator except one, and he had grown quite fat and white haired. I, of course, have not aged at all.

I met one of Teddy Kennedy's sisters that same year. Patricia Kennedy had been married to the British actor, Peter Lawford, who was part of the "rat pack" that included Sammy Davis, Jr., Frank Sinatra, and Dean Martin. Pat Kennedy was divorced from Peter Lawford at the time she arrived in Madrid in 1966. Ambassador Duke was out of town and Minister William Walker, the second in command of the embassy, asked me to go to dinner with him and Pat Kennedy and the boyfriend accompanying her. It was a strange evening. One thing making it stranger is that Pat Kennedy was wearing the shortest mini-skirt I had ever seen. I had nothing against mini-skirts on women of any age, but there was something absurd about the way her mini-skirt fit. She had very much a little girl look. Her underpants were on full display. I expected her at any moment to stick her thumb in her mouth or pull a lollypop out of her pocketbook.

Which might not have been unexpected given the shallowness of her conversation. Walker and I continued to sound her out on the ideas of the day, but she seemed to know, and have views on, nothing at all. Boredom is a sensation I rarely experience, but I experienced it that evening. And the fellow Pat Kennedy was with didn't add anything to the conversation—which increasingly became more and more between Walker and me. The next day Walker stopped me in the embassy hallway and said, "Did you believe those two? Dumb as posts."

Nevertheless, in my youthful idealism, I still clung to the belief that the Kennedys were somehow

"Senator Edward Kennedy on the left, the author on the right, at the program at the University of Madrid."

superhuman or, at least, better than the rest of us. But perhaps it was only the men who got the opportunity to project that image. They certainly got all the attention. I don't know if Pat Kennedy was typical of the Kennedy women, but given the extremely sexist environment in which they were raised, perhaps the women didn't thrive because they knew from birth that they were of little value except, perhaps, as ornaments and to breed.

Of course, Jacqueline Kennedy was not born a Kennedy, so she may have escaped some of that family's deleterious effects on its women. Jacqueline too came to Madrid at the invitation of Angier Biddle Duke, and he had a reception in her honor to which I was invited. I don't know if I can fully communicate the reverence with which I approached meeting her. She was the widow of our heroic, handsome, and martyred president. She was the embodiment of Camelot. If someone had told me that she was the Virgin Mary, even as someone who doesn't believe in such things, I would have accepted it. She certainly was the American Madonna, and I don't mean the dancing-singing one of later years. For five years in a row she had been voted the most popular woman in the world. The Jacqueline Kennedy of that moment in Madrid was someone I worshipped. If not the American Madonna or the Virgin Mary, she was certainly the closest thing America has ever produced to a goddess.

I would have given anything to meet Jacqueline Kennedy. And now, here I was indeed meeting her, and we were standing alone together at the ambassador's reception, and I was struck dumb. I was meeting the most famous woman in the world and I would have wanted to tell her that I adored her, that I would do anything for her, that I would have died for her. What I actually did say I cannot recall. Something stupid, for sure. I remember only her smile and soft "Thank you."

I met three Kennedys during my years in Madrid. And they had a lot to do with my growing up.

Meeting them helped me to stop idolizing them or anyone else for that matter. I came to see them as human beings, flawed like the rest of us. Like other people there was much that was admirable about them, much that was not. Why do we always have to pigeonhole people as either black or white? We may all be different shades of gray.

It is said that maturity is all about recognizing limitations. Recognizing the limitations of the Kennedys helped me to forgive myself for some of my own. Still, I miss the Kennedys. They made a lot of us feel good about our country.

# The Bombs of Palomares and the Casa Americana

ON JANUARY 17, 1966 I sat, disconsolate, in my office at the American Embassy. For six months I had been overseeing the creation of a new Casa Americana, the American cultural center in Madrid. The old Casa had been at the back of the Embassy, but it had been decided to turn it into the ambassador's residence and recreate the Casa across the Avenida Castellana in an ornate palace that once belonged to a Spanish aristocratic family. The ambassador's previous residence had been elsewhere in Madrid. There had been demonstrations there recently—oranges thrown, broken windows—and it had been decided, for security reasons, to place the official residence within the walled embassy compound at Serrano, 75.

Also, it was thought the Casa Americana would be more effective away from the embassy—purely cultural, divorced from political, economic, and military affairs. I liked that idea a lot. There would be a better chance of demonstrating that we Americans were not complete barbarians as some Spanish intellectuals believed.

One could understand some of their antipathy. The United States was, after all, intimately con-

A concert of American folk music held in the garden of the Casa Americana. The author is on foot on the right.

nected with the Franco government militarily—with air bases at Morón (near Seville) and Torrejón (outside Madrid) and a nuclear submarine base at Rota (near Cadiz). My Spanish friends tended to admire our popular culture but not our politics. Stereotypes of Americans also abounded. I would sometimes receive the left-handed compliment that I was *simpatico* because I was "not like other Americans." Inquiring what other Americans were like, I would invariably be told: "blond, fat, and stupid." It was my job as a cultural attaché to convince Spaniards otherwise.

Why was I down in the dumps that day in January, 1966? A new diplomatic officer had joined the embassy cultural section. He outranked me and announced that he would direct the Casa Americana. I had done all the preparatory work; he would have all the fun. He would get the luxurious office that had been created—I thought for me—with its own balcony overlooking the Avenida Castellana and an elaborate, carved marble fireplace. I would remain within my ordinary embassy office and, enmeshed in the bureaucracy, push paper instead of running my own shop. I was angry; it wasn't fair. Directing a cultural center is like managing an institute of some sort on a university campus, a way of being something like a "professor" in the government. There I could have freely hung out with Spanish writers and artists and intellectuals instead of the boring people diplomats often must deal with in their everyday work. Who would have suspected that my pleasure in my work was about to be enhanced by an event of sheer horror?

At 10:22 that morning a United States Air Force B-52 bomber collided with a KC-135 tanker over the Spanish coast. The tanker exploded in a ball of flame, and all four airmen aboard were lost. Three of the seven airmen on the B-52 were also killed. The others ejected and floated down by parachute into the sea, where they were picked up by Spanish fishermen, or onto the town of Palomares. The four hydrogen bombs the B-52 was carrying, each seventy-five times more powerful than the bombs dropped on Hiroshima and Nagasaki, but fortunately unarmed, also floated down, supported by their parachutes. Three bombs landed on Palomares. The other's whereabouts would remain unknown for many weeks.

Palomares is located in one of the most isolated corners of the Province of Almeria. In 1966, no paved roads reached it. An arid, dusty town of 250 families, mostly tomato farmers, there wasn't, in 1966, a single telephone in Palomares. Isolating it further, some of the debris descending from the two smashed planes, miraculously not hitting any houses or people, severed the power lines to the town so that, in addition to everything else, Palomares was temporarily without electricity.

What were these two American planes doing 31,000 feet above Spain? The world would soon learn that the United States sent squadrons of three B-52s twenty-four hours a day, 365 days a year, towards the borders of the Soviet Union. A squadron would fly in circles for some hours in what was popularly known as the "fail-safe" position. Relieved by a new squadron it would turn around and head back to the United States. These missions were considered necessary at the time under the Cold War principle of mutual deterrence vis-à-vis the Soviets. They would end in a few years when missiles replaced bombers. And now, thank goodness, many of the missiles have been deactivated too.

The bombers needed to have their tanks topped up en route to the Soviet Union and totally refueled as they limped back to the United States. This particular squadron, which had left an air base in North Carolina, had been refueled on the way over by a tanker from Torrejón and, on the way back, was about to be refueled by a tanker from Morón. Tanker planes, flying fuel tanks, customarily rendezvoused with B-52s at the edge of the Spanish coast.

The people of Palomares were used to seeing these planes several times a day high above the town. A B-52 would slow to 250 miles per hour and slide under a tanker. The tanker would send a long boom down into the B-52, fill its tanks, and then break off contact. This operation had been successively concluded thousands of times. But on January 17, 1966 a B-52 had apparently come up too fast under the tanker. There was a collision and, as the startled people of Palomares would say for years afterwards, "fire rained down from the sky."

When the accident occurred, a colleague of mine, a young political attaché at the embassy, received the news in a telephone call from an air force officer at Torrejón Air Base. He ran into the office of Angier Biddle Duke, but the ambassador was downtown delivering a speech to the Spanish-American Chamber of Commerce. The young diplomat rushed there and stood in the back of the hall frantically waving his arms, but he couldn't get the ambassador's attention, and, when he did, the ambassador, annoyed, ignored him. Finally, he rushed up onto the platform and whispered in the ambassador's ear, "Four of our hydrogen bombs have just fallen on Spain." The ambassador gasped, stopped speaking in mid-sentence, and the two men rushed out without a word to those who had been listening to the speech.

A businessman friend later told me that people there thought President Lyndon Johnson had been assassinated. After all, John Kennedy had been assassinated only a bit more than two years before, and the shock from that had yet to wear off. Perhaps, they thought, assassinating presidents was becoming a habit.

Ambassador Duke decided to immediately call on the Spanish foreign minister. But, on arrival at the ministry, he discovered the minister was away at a funeral. Duke finally met with a lesser functionary and was able to officially report the accident and assure the Spanish government that the United States had not attacked Spain with nuclear weapons. One can only imagine Duke's words: "Sorry for dropping four hydrogen bombs on you, boys. Not to worry."

Later that day the ambassador called all embassy staff into an emergency meeting in the top floor conference room. That was when I found out about Palomares. I had read the 1962 novel *Fail-Safe* by Eugene Burdick and Harvey Wheeler and seen Stanley Kubrick's 1964 black comedy, *Dr. Strangelove,* both of which deal with similar nuclear events, but this was real.

The ambassador said, "We are in deep trouble. Did any of you know about these B-52s refueling above the Spanish coast, because I sure didn't?"

No one raised their hands.

The ambassador's secretary got some Air Force general at Strategic Air Command, Omaha, on the speaker phone. "Why didn't I know this refueling operation was going on?" the ambassador demanded to know.

"Top secret," the general responded.

Duke, normally a smooth, easygoing guy, got red in the face. "Whatya mean 'top secret?' I'm the ambassador. I'm the president's personal representative in Spain. Who should know if I don't know?"

"I can't tell you that, Sir," the general intoned.

"Well," said Duke, "if you can't tell me, you can go fuck yourself." Never before or after did I hear the ambassador speak in that fashion.

The tension in the room was thick. Nothing in the world was more important at that moment than what was going on at Palomares and at the embassy. History was being made, and I was excited to be part of it—and scared. Scared that, no matter what, America's relationship with Spain would thenceforth be more difficult and its position in the world seriously compromised. And scared personally too. It felt like World War III had just begun.

I also thought, Casa Americana or no Casa Americana, those bombs were surely going to undermine my work. I wondered whether I would still be welcome at Spanish universities and in cultural circles around the country. It would be difficult celebrating American culture in Spain when we had just dropped four hydrogen bombs on the country.

Fortunately, as I would learn, nuclear bombs are inert unless armed. To arm such a device six distinct procedures must be followed, and they can only be done in a certain sequence by two designated airmen aboard a bomber and only on the direct orders of the President of the United States. The codes for doing so changed daily. They were in the little black bag carried by an Air Force officer who accompanied the president everywhere. However, each bomb also has a small charge of conventional explosives to initiate the nuclear fission process. These conventional explosives will go off if a bomb comes down more rapidly than it should and strikes the earth.

One of the bombs floated down on its parachute and was later found intact in Palomares. But the parachutes of two of them were partially burned in the air disaster, so the bombs came down rapidly. When they landed at Palomares their conventional explosives went off. No one was hurt in these explosions—though one man said he was knocked off his feet. But the explosions cracked those two bombs open, releasing their plutonium into the air in small black clouds. Plutonium is one of the deadliest substances on earth. If one inhales a tiny amount death is certain within days. Even minimal exposure will almost guarantee lethal cancers years later. Luckily, a strong wind was blowing from an unaccustomed direction that day. It apparently dispersed the plutonium away from the people of Palomares and widely out over the Mediterranean.

For three days the combined forces of the United States Air Force, the American Embassy, and the Spanish government kept the Palomares story bottled up. The town was cordoned off, with only authorized people allowed into and out of Palomares. Nuclear experts from both countries arrived on the scene. Military personnel in the hundreds came to Palomares, most assigned to systematically walk every inch of the town and its surrounding fields with Geiger Counters or to collect debris from the two planes. The better part of both wings of the B-52 had landed—minus the motors but largely intact—one in a tomato field, the other in shallow water just off Palomares.

One of them would end up as "sculpture" on the wall of the dining room of a hotel in the hill town of Mojacar, a few kilometers down the coast from Palomares. I vacationed with my family in Mojacar in 1972, and we dined one evening at the hotel with that wing hanging over us. One of my children started crying. He was afraid the wing would fall on him, so we asked to change to a table some distance away. Today, the hotel is no longer there, and no one in Mojacar seems to know what happened to the wing.

By January 19th an enterprising newsman from Madrid had made his way into Palomares, and the next day the world knew what was going on there. Palomares would be the number one story in world media for weeks to come. Soviet media, in particular, would have a field day with the story, accusing the United States of intentionally dropping nuclear bombs on Spain.

The world's attention was focused on the missing bomb, not the radiation issue, which was of more immediate concern to American and Spanish officials. Still, both governments were unwilling for six weeks to officially admit that one of the bombs was lost. The following colloquy, half-Orwell, half-Woody Allen, took place at a press conference held by a United States Air Force officer:

Reporter: "Tell me, any sign of the bomb?"

Air Force Spokesman: "What bomb?"

Reporter: "Well, you know, the thing you're looking for?"

Air Force Spokesman: "You know perfectly well we're not looking for any bomb. Just looking for debris."

Reporter: "All right, any signs of what you say is not a bomb?"

Air Force Spokesman: "If you put it that way, I can tell you that there is no sign of the thing that is not a bomb."

Because of concern over radiation, it was almost preferable that attention was diverted to the missing bomb. The people of Palomares were not allowed to harvest their tomatoes and other crops, nor to sell the tomatoes that had already been harvested and were in the warehouse. Six million kilos of tomatoes had been harvested the previous year. Now the current tomatoes and other crops rotted. One farmer refused to evacuate his field. He said to an American airman, "I don't know what this radiation is. All I know is that this is my field and I refuse to go. I've got beans to pick." The Spanish national police, the Guardia Civil, was called in to escort the protesting farmer off his land.

It would be years before the tomatoes, milk, and other agricultural products of Palomares would be entirely welcome in Madrid, Barcelona, and elsewhere in Europe. Some joked that they had a certain glow. This was the first known example of radioactive contamination of an inhabited area during peacetime since the beginning of the nuclear age.

While the people of Palomares were told that they would be fully reimbursed for their losses by the American government, and eventually were, meanwhile they had nothing to do. The farmers stood about aimlessly. At first they could not even feed their livestock, who, because of radiation fears, were proscribed from grazing in their accustomed fields. Even the fishermen from Garrucha, a town close to Palomares, would not be allowed to put to sea. Needless to say, the bars in both towns did a lot of business.

Most important was the health of the residents of the town. Urine tests had immediately been administered to every man, woman, and child. In test after test they showed a high level of contamination, even those whose immediate surroundings at the time the bombs came down showed no contamination at all. Finally, it was determined that the collection bottles themselves were contaminated. Once the bottles were cleansed of radiation, new urine samples showed no human contamination at all. Routine urinalyses of the residents of Palomares would, nevertheless, continue for many years afterwards and, it is rumored, continue to this day.

Six hundred and forty acres of Palomares would be bulldozed, including all the crops growing on them. This material would be pulverized and packed into 5,500 specially commissioned 55 gallon drums, loaded onto a ship, and taken across the Atlantic to an abandoned quarry in South Carolina, where it was sealed in. Fresh topsoil would be brought in to replace it and new houses constructed for the residents of the town. It is ironic that virtually all of the original Palomares is actually to be found today in the United States.

With the radiation issue seemingly under control, the missing bomb became the center of attention. There was no sign of it on land, so the emphasis switched to looking for it at sea. A fleet of some fifteen American naval vessels—including minesweepers and other ships with up-to-date sonar gear—assembled with 2,200 naval personnel, including 130 frogmen. Also available, having been flown over to Spain, were mini-submarines, straight out of Jules Verne, such as the Alvin that were capable of dives to great depths. The navy, its efforts hampered by the high winds and rough water of late winter, began combing the bottom of the Mediterranean over an area 12 miles out to sea and 10 miles along the coast, or 120 square miles, a vast area.

A Spanish fisherman, Francisco Simó Orts—who had picked up Major Larry Messinger, the pilot of the B-52, after he had been treading water for forty-five minutes—said he knew exactly where the bomb was, five and one-half miles out in the Mediterranean. But no one gave much credence to his story. Even if, as he claimed, he had seen it come down, how could a man at sea remember where on the water a bomb had fallen? Of course, as we would eventually learn, fishermen and others who go to sea regularly in a particular area know exactly where they are in the water at all times, much as the rest of us do on land.

As the United States Navy slowly reduced the area to be searched, another issue arose. What of the vital tourism in this whole region of Spain, famous for its beaches and resorts. It had already been determined there were no dangerous levels of radiation in the sea, but would the world believe that, especially with a lost bomb somewhere under the waves?

Ambassador Duke and Spanish Minister of Information and Tourism, Manuel Fraga Iribañe, decided to go swimming in the Mediterranean on March 8, 1966 to prove that the waters were not dangerous to health. Luckily, I had been sent down to Palomares as a courier during the night. This was not part of my normal embassy duties, but no diplomatic courier was then available and important papers had just been flown in from the White House related to Palomares that the ambassador needed to see. A briefcase was attached to my wrist with a device very much like a handcuff and chain. I was given an embassy car, and my driver drove through the night. I tried to sleep in the back seat, but the briefcase to which I was chained and my chafed wrist allowed me little rest.

I arrived in Palomares early in the morning. It looked like a war zone. American and Spanish military milled about. Ships were just off shore. Helicopters roared overhead, causing cows and sheep to bolt in terror, running this way and that. I soon learned that Ambassador Duke was not in Palomares but down the coast at the parador, or government hotel, on the beach below Mojacar, where he and staff from the embassy, some with wives and children, had spent the night. There were going to be two swim-ins. Duke would swim that morning at Mojacar, and Fraga, who was otherwise occupied, would join him in the water that afternoon at Palomares itself.

Arriving in Mojacar, I was relieved of the briefcase just in time to see the ambassador stride out of the parador in a bathing suit. Surrounded by staff and the international press, he walked very erect and dignified down the sand to the water's edge. The air temperature was 58 degrees Fahrenheit. Lord only knows what the water temperature was after the long winter.

When Duke plunged into the sea there was confusion on the beach. If the ambassador was in the water, did it not behoove his staff to join him—in the interest of not compromising our careers if nothing else? Some embassy personnel were prepared for the occasion with bathing suits. They ran into the water after Duke. Having just come from Madrid, I was the only one on the beach in a suit, so I thought I was safe from criticism if I didn't enter the water. But soon, other embassy staff were tearing off their clothes and running into the ocean in their underpants. One discovered immediately who among long term colleagues favored boxer shorts and who favored briefs, who was in good shape, and who flabby. Lots of surprises there.

Now I no longer had an excuse, so I quickly disrobed, laying my best wool suit on the sand. I had considerable difficulty with my tie. I finally tore it off, popping a button from my button down collar. I ran into the water as quickly as I could, partly because I was the last one in but, also, because I was not wearing a pair of my best underpants. In fact, the pair I was wearing was torn in—shall we say?—unacceptable, or at least embarrassing, places. I cursed myself for not having thrown it out long ago. Damn it, there were photographers on the beach! And women!

It was freezing, but those of us in the water splashed each other and laughed, as if on holiday. We were relieved when the ambassador decided he had had enough and headed out of the water, the rest of us following quickly up onto the beach. Maids from the hotel were waiting with towels. I grabbed two, wrapping the first around my waist, before using the other to dry off. Elegantly dressed waiters from the parador were on the beach with shots of cognac on little round trays, compliments of the house. We seemed to be having an impromptu cocktail party on that chilly beach.

I was not present when Duke and Fraga had their swim-in that afternoon; I was on my way back to Madrid. Because so much embassy staff was down at Palomares, there was only a skeleton crew in Madrid; I was needed there. The afternoon swim was the one that produced one of the most famous photographs of the 1960s: Duke and Fraga frolicking in the water. The event was dubbed by the press, "The Splash Heard Round the World." But it was the morning swim-in that embassy staff would best remember, especially those of us who swam in our underpants. Not many years before I had been captain of my college swim team, but no race I ever participated in, even the time I broke the team and pool record, ever equaled the excitement of that March swim in the Mediterranean.

Meanwhile, the search for the missing bomb continued at sea, and American naval personnel, perhaps out of desperation, finally decided that Francisco Simó Orts' story was worthy of attention. On March 15 the bomb was located 2,550 feet below the very spot he had seen it enter the water from the deck of his boat, the Agustin y Rosa. Ever since then, Simó has been something of a folk hero in Spain known as Paco de la Bomba (Paco, The Bomb Guy). Paco is the standard nickname for Francisco.

On March 24th, an attempt was made to haul the bomb to the surface. Almost immediately the cable snapped and the bomb again descended to the bottom. The Navy was not just dragging up a 5,000 pound bomb but the 20,000 pounds of water in the deployed parachute, and pulling it up with only one cable attached to the parachute.

It took days to relocate the bomb. It was now at a point 250 feet deeper. More serious: it was on a slippery slope close to a crevice 3,000 feet deep. If the bomb ever fell into that crevice there would be no way to get it out. While the Alvin was capable of descending to 6,000 feet, the crevice was too narrow to admit any submersible.

This time the Alvin attempted to attach multiple lines to the parachute, but, before it could do so, it became entangled in its shrouds. The two man crew was in danger of dying down there as their oxygen expired. The Alvin finally freed itself but nearly rammed the bomb. Had it been hit, the conventional dynamite charge might have exploded, destroying the Alvin and its crew and spreading the bomb's plutonium into the sea.

Two days later an unmanned device, the CURV, was sent down. It too got entangled in the parachute, but not before attaching several lines to it. It was decided to try to winch up the bomb and parachute and simultaneously, use the power of the entangled CURV vehicle to help in the salvage attempt. After one hour and seventeen minutes, bomb, parachute, and vehicle had risen to 100 feet below the surface. Frogmen met it and disentangled the CURV from the parachute. On April 7, 1966, at 8:40 a.m. in the morning, the ten-foot long, twenty inches in diameter hydrogen bomb was hoisted aboard the USS Petrel. The casing of this bomb and of the other bomb that did not crack open upon landing on Palomares, are on display at the National Museum of Nuclear Science and History in Albuquerque, New Mexico if any readers would like to see them.

The feature film, *Men of Honor* (2000), has scenes dramatizing the recovery of the fourth Palomares bomb, though a U.S. Navy diver, played by Cuba Gooding, Jr., comes upon the bomb while walking on the bottom of the ocean, impossible be-

The missing, fourth hydrogen bomb finally lifted from the sea floor of the Mediterranean and displayed aboard a United States Naval vessel, the USS Petrel.

cause the bomb was at a depth where no diver could survive and, as the reader already knows, this was not how the bomb was discovered and recovered.

Ambassador Duke argued that no one would believe the bomb had been found unless it was displayed to the world. The military felt this would compromise security. The White House was brought in to decide, and Duke prevailed. The international press was invited the next day to photograph the bomb aboard the ship with navy personnel proudly standing about. April 8 was Good Friday. It would be a very good Friday indeed. Eighty-one days had passed between the January 17th collision and the display of the fourth bomb.

During that time our entire embassy thought of virtually nothing but Palomares. This was not just a military but a political crisis of international magnitude. All the embassy's resources were devoted to minimizing the damage to the reputation of the United States and to reassuring the Spanish public. There were occasional demonstrations outside the embassy. Colleagues worked round the clock under great stress. Even my immediate superior, who had said that he would be director of the Casa Americana, had been pressed into action.

Which is how I became Director of the Casa Americana. With everyone worrying about the bombs, culture wasn't high on anyone's list. Nevertheless, Ambassador Duke attended the Casa's inaugural festivities. Minister Fraga attended one of its first public events. This was just after their swim in the Mediterranean but before the missing bomb had been definitively located and lifted from the sea floor. I suspect each man considered a cultural event a welcome diversion from Palomares and the immense embarrassment it caused both governments.

The Casa inaugurated, we proceeded to offer non stop events—jazz concerts, poetry readings, lectures, exhibits. At first, attendance was sparse. Few Spaniards wanted to associate with the United States at that moment. But after the missing bomb was brought to the surface attendance increased dramatically.

Two years later, shortly after I left the Spain embassy, someone put a bomb in the Casa Americana. I read about it in the American press and joked that certain Spaniards missed me so much that this was their way of expressing their displeasure at my absence. Considerable damage was done, and a wall of

Ambassador Angier Biddle Duke on the right extending his hand and the author on the left at the inauguration of the Casa Americana.

books fell on the woman who had been my librarian. She was injured but survived. That would have been an irony: to be a librarian and be killed by books. Some years later the Casa Americana on the Avenida Castellana was abandoned and a new one opened close to the University of Madrid.

Whenever I am in Madrid I pass by the place where my Casa Americana once stood. There is a skyscraper there now, the headquarters of an insurance company, I believe. At that very spot I once had a little cultural empire. And it was given to me by four nuclear bombs.

Postscript. I am a bit embarrassed because when I first wrote this book, and it appeared in Spanish, I did not know of certain events concerning Palomares that have taken place in the past year or so. In 2009, the mayor of the little town of Palomares proposed the creation of a museum, a theme park, or both devoted to the incidents of 1966. However quixotic, he thought it would attract tourists and other visitors to the area. There was already a street in tiny Palomares named January 17, 1966. One of the main things the mayor wanted to put on display was the swimsuit Manuel Fraga wore for his dip with Angier Biddle Duke that fateful day in March 1966. Fraga's swimsuit was reportedly still at his home in the Galicia region of Spain. I could also supply a pair of torn underpants to the mayor of Palomares should he want it—though not the originals.

There was also word in 2009 that the Walt Disney Company had plans for a film to be titled "Muchas Gracias, Bob Oppenheimer" (the scientist, Robert Oppenheimer, is known as the father of the hydrogen bomb). The film would be about an American serviceman who meets and falls in love with a girl from Palomares because of the accident of 1966. Palomares villagers were hoping the film, at least in part, would be shot on location—bringing much revenue to the area. Were the film actually made, the world would know about Palomares once again.

In 2010, Palomares was again back in the news. It had been discovered that in a low lying area of the town deadly radiation remains. Apparently, the cleanup of 1966 was not complete. Either someone made a mistake or got lazy, but there is, in this area, plutonium just under the surface of soil that had been used as fill. This location has now been cordoned off and, as I write this, the American and Spanish governments are in negotiations as to just how to deal with the problem. While fencing the area effectively keeps people out of it, it doesn't stop small animals such as rabbits from burrowing and otherwise spreading about some of the radiation. Not to mention that this area was not closed off to people for the previous forty-four years.

My hunch is that with the rediscovery of radiation in Palomares, the mayor's plans for a museum and theme park and Disney's plans for a film will be dropped. Palomares is unlikely to ever attract tourists, nor would a romantic comedy make sense in an area where there is still deadly radiation.

For the present there is a more immediate concern: the farmers of Palomares are again having difficulty marketing their tomatoes.

# Afterword: When I Left the Diplomatic Service

B EING OVERSEAS and in the diplomatic service—and serving in countries that were extremely right wing; not just Spain but Argentina as well—I had all but missed the excitement and turmoil of the Sixties in America. My Sixties would have to wait until it was almost the Seventies.

For reasons discussed in the introduction to this book—related to my Viet Nam assignment—I resigned from the federal government in late March, 1968, taking a job in higher education administration New Jersey's state capitol, Trenton. Ralph Dungan, a member of the "Irish Mafia" in the Kennedy White House, was, after a stint as Ambassador to Chile, now Chancellor of Higher Education, and he hired me as his Executive Assistant. Lyndon Johnson wanted Kennedy's guys anywhere but near the White House. I had met Ralph in Argentina years before when he was part of the American delegation to the inauguration of a new Argentine president— one who didn't last long. The Argentines were forever inaugurating a new president. In the two years I was there they had three revolutions and two coups. Spain was a dictatorship, but it was calm.

The new job paid well, but I longed to be back in Spain. Not just to be back there but out of the United States. The United States I returned to after my years abroad was a different place than the one I had left. I felt like a stranger in my own country. Everything seemed too intense.

The first thing Dungan asked me to do was to represent him at a meeting with a group of black faculty and students who were demanding a decent slice of the academic pie. They were right, of course, but I didn't see it that way then. They seemed so radical to a person who had just left the white gloved diplomatic service, where people rarely raised their voices and everything was, well, genteel. I didn't understand why these blacks were so angry. Half an hour into the meeting they were turning their anger on me. Hey, I wanted to say, *I've been involved in Civil Rights all my life. I hung out with Martin Luther King in Madrid. I'm one of the good guys.*

Maybe so, but if I was one of the good guys, I was now one of the *dumb* good guys. The country had moved on, and I hadn't been at home to move on with it. My "wisdom" on race relations had been formed in the decade in which I grew up, the 1950s, and I suppose a large part of me was still back there. I left that meeting feeling emotionally bruised and unjustly maligned.

A few days later, on April 4, 1968, Martin Luther King was assassinated in Memphis, Tennessee. I learned of this in a barbershop in Trenton into which I had wandered when I saw the swirling red and white barber pole. Neighborhood retired, white men seemed to use the place as a hangout. Some of them, who had just come from the bar next door, were obviously drunk. When the news came on the radio about Martin, I sat there stunned, then doubly horrified when everyone in the barber shop cheered. "Glad somebody finally got that nigger," one man said.

I couldn't believe it. The greatest American of those times had just been killed and these men were happy?! And not just a very great American, but someone I loved. I didn't know whether to cry or start hitting people. But my barber was just then shaving the back of my neck with an open straight razor, and there were seven or eight of these guys. Still, I couldn't stay there another minute. My haircut only half over, I tore off the cloth, threw five dollars down by the cash register (Yes, that's what haircuts cost then; and I was damned if I would tip), grabbed my jacket, and walked out of there without a word. Now I understood better what had been bugging those black university people at that meeting a few days earlier because it was not only bugging me too; I was enraged.

What is it about April? I wondered. Lincoln had also been assassinated in April. At home, that evening I got out Whitman's *Leaves of Grass* and read a poem he wrote in response to Lincoln's death, "When Lilacs Last in the Dooryard Bloom'd." I've never felt quite the same about lilacs since. April was indeed "the cruelest month," as T. S. Eliot, who also mentioned lilacs, wrote in "The Wasteland." April: so much beauty, so much death.

Years later the world would learn that the FBI, directed by the infamous J. Edgar Hoover, had kept a thick dossier on Martin and would regularly attempt to blackmail him into compromising his civil rights efforts. Hoover considered King "the most dangerous man in America"—which I suppose he was if one considers meaningful change dangerous. I am not much of a conspiracy theorist but, to this day, I believe there was more behind Martin Luther King's murder than the infamy of a single, not particularly racist, crackpot, James Earl Ray.

Riots broke out across the country in response to Martin's murder, and they were, of course, accompanied by the growing rage against the Vietnam War. Not long after, in June, Bobby Kennedy was also assassinated. What was it with this country of mine? It seemed like a madhouse. When I left it had seemed a reasonably peaceful place. Then John Kennedy was killed and my youth began slipping away. Martin's and Bobby's deaths finished it off. You grow up when there's no one left to idolize.

When I entered the diplomatic service, the United States was all Doris Day and Bing Crosby. Now it was Janis Joplin and Bob Dylan and Jimmy Hendrix's violent version of "The Star Spangled Banner." While in graduate school at the University of Minnesota years before I had often walked past a little off campus coffee shop called The Ten O'Clock Scholar and heard what I considered infernal howling coming from within. "What a loser that guy must be," I said to myself. That guy turned out to be

Bob Dylan. It wasn't till I was out of the diplomatic service and back home that I was capable of appreciating his genius.

America was going through a revolution, and I got re-Americanized so quickly that soon I was immersed, if not involved in that revolution. After a year with the Department of Higher Education I was hired by Rutgers University as a dean. Though this wasn't my title, I was, in effect, the Dean of Hassles. My first day on the job was January 20, 1969, the same day Richard Nixon began his presidency. I'd like to believe I fared better in my job than he did in his.

The campus was ablaze—figuratively and sometimes literally, students throwing Molotov cocktails at the ROTC building when they weren't chaining themselves together inside the president's office. Coming from a political background, I was hired to negotiate with the radicals—to somehow keep students and faculty operating within the law while defending freedom of speech to state legislators who contemplated closing down the university.

I hadn't gone to Vietnam, but Vietnam had come to me. I probably saw more action as a dean on the Rutgers campus in those days than I would have as a diplomat in Vietnam. I had, it seemed, gone from the proverbial frying pan into the fire.

I didn't deal with the official student government in my new job. They were no more a part of the tail end of the Sixties than I was. I dealt with the students and faculty who were, in effect, demanding radical change. It wasn't just the war and civil rights.

Some faculty were demanding an end to grading. Students were walking around campus with raised fists shouting, "Student power." A group of black students one evening passed through the food line in a university cafeteria and then threw their laden trays up in the air, everything crashing and breaking, the food spreading everywhere in a gooey mess. Soon the Puerto Rican students were also on the march. Then it would be the women. Then the gays.

My second day on the job I made up my mind to seek out a certain young woman who was known to be the leader of the radicals. But before I could find her she found me. My new secretary came in and told me of a strange looking student outside who wanted to see me. Was I available to see her? I went into the anteroom and here was that very girl, her wild hair wrapped in a large red bandana, a big, brass peace symbol around her neck, and a T-shirt that asked, a reference to the Vietnam War I assumed, "Burn Any Babies Today?" She very clearly wasn't wearing a bra, part of the struggle for freedom, I supposed.

Her jeans were as interesting as her T-shirt. They consisted of more holes than cloth. All the time I was in Spain friends had asked if I could somehow get them jeans; they weren't sold yet in Spain. Now they are an international uniform. These friends didn't have in mind jeans like those this girl was wearing. Of course, these days such denim pants are very fashionable. They're called "Stressed Jeans" and cost a fortune, sometimes as much as $275, but that girl's jeans weren't stressed, just worn out.

I invited the young woman into my office. She sat down but looked uncomfortable.

"What's the matter?" I asked.

"Let's go somewhere else to talk," she said.

I wanted to know why. "Because your office is probably bugged," she said.

"My office isn't bugged," I insisted. "Universities don't bug offices." Perhaps one worried about such things while serving in an embassy, but in a university?

"Boy, are you naïve," she said. Maybe I was, I thought. Or was it just the paranoia of the times? She suggested we go outside and talk on the big grassy recreation field behind the administration building. "They couldn't bug us there," she said, "unless you're wearing a wire."

I assured her I was not. Her thinking I might be was a sign of the times.

"Swear?" she asked.

"Swear," I replied. But I thought it best to open my jacket, pull my shirt out of my pants, and empty my pockets onto my desk.

We went outside onto that large, empty field. It was an exceptionally warm January day.

"I hear you left the diplomatic thing because of Vietnam," she said.

"Something like that," I replied.

This seemed to immeasurably increase her confidence in me. She took out a joint, lit it, took a hit, and passed it to me. I had never seen marijuana before, much less tried it.

That was my moment of truth. If I had refused the marijuana, she wouldn't have trusted me. But what if some of my new colleagues were looking out the window just at that moment, wondering what this brand new dean was doing walking on the field with this strange looking, half naked student? And what were those two smoking?

"Screw it," I said to myself and took a big hit on the joint she was holding out to me. And unlike Bill Clinton, I admit it: I inhaled. Being an amateur, I had a coughing fit, but in a few moments I was feeling devil-may-care wonderful.

Soon the girl and I were skipping about the field, holding hands and giggling. We found ourselves agreeing about absolutely everything—from politics to the meaning of life—and in the ensuing months remained friends and worked a lot of things out. I think that marijuana I smoked that day ended up doing not only me but Rutgers University a lot of good.

On that field I had passed some kind of test. It wasn't just that the leader of the radical students now trusted me. It was that, though I continued to miss Spain, I had reentered my own culture. Diplomats, to keep from "going native," come home every few years for a month's vacation or even a Washington assignment. Even though my decision to come home was, following my resignation, of my own volition, I suppose I had, in my affection for Spain, gone a bit native. My country, the country I had represented overseas, was, until that moment, still more foreign to me than Spain. But now America fascinated me.

The country was rife with dangers but also with potential, and I had been thrust into the middle of it all. For better or worse, it was once again my country.

# About the Author

MICHAEL AARON ROCKLAND is professor of American studies at Rutgers University. His early career, in the United States Diplomatic Service, inspired this memoir. It is his thirteenth book and, in a somewhat different form, was first published in Spanish by the Biblioteca Javier Coy of the University of Valencia Press.

In his writing, Rockland moves back and forth between memoir, fiction, journalism, and history. Five of his books have won prizes or received similar recognition, including *New York Times'* "Notable Book of the Year" and *Washington Post's* "Fifty Best Books of the Year." A book he co-wrote, *Looking for America on the New Jersey Turnpike*, was chosen by the New Jersey State Library as one of the "Ten Best Books Ever Written on New Jersey or by a New Jerseyan." Two other books received the prize of the New Jersey Studies Alliance.

Rockland has also worked in television and filmmaking and is a regular contributor to several magazines, most regularly *New Jersey Monthly*. He has won five major teaching awards, including the national teaching award in American Studies.

## Also by *Michael Aaron Rockland*
from Hansen Publishing Group

# Stones

A sneaky and beautiful little masterpiece – sneaky because its disarmingly simple premise of a single day spent visiting graves manages somehow to communicate the endless complexity of one Jewish-American family over the span of nearly a century, and beautiful because Michael Rockland tells his story with a generous, generous heart.

—Tom De Haven, author of *It's Superman*

STONES is a novel simultaneously serious and comic. It takes place in one day as its protagonist, Jack Berke, accompanies his aged mother Rachel to visit the family graves in Brooklyn, Queens, and further out on Long Island. As Jack negotiates the congested expressways from cemetery to cemetery, he contemplates the tombstones, the lives of family members who lie under them, the stones that, according to Jewish custom, he places on those tombstones, and the stone that has for a lifetime resided in his own heart.

Paperback $14.95 • ISBN 978-1-60182-300-7 • 140 pages
eBook $2.99 • available for the Kindle, the Nook, and the iPad

**B ROCKLAND**

**Rockland, Michael Aaron,**

**An American diplomat in Franco Spain**

WARREN TWP LIBRARY
42 MOUNTAIN BLVD

JAN 3 1 2014

WARREN, NJ 07059
908-754-5554

CPSIA information can be obtained at www.ICGtesting.com
Printed in the USA
LVOW12s1922281013

358942LV00020B/935/P